MYSTIC

AND THE SECRET
OF

HAPPINESS

Anne-Claire Szubaniska

Mystic and the Secret of Happiness

ACAM PUBLISHING

ISBN: 978-0-9983848-3-2

Cover by Antoine Mainguy and Lhor

www.mysticthebook.com

ACAM Publishing is a DBA of ACAM Enterprises LLC, New York

*To my mother
and my grand-parents,
Papi and Miman.*

PREFACE

The story you're about to read is something I've lived with for a long time. It was in my head long before I even wrote a single word, and existed in many different iterations. The ideas it contains, and the journey the main character undertakes are very near and dear to my heart. If you've read the 'About the Author' section of my website, you know I suffered from depression and anorexia, and it took me many years to overcome them. Looking back, I wish I'd had some sort of guideline which would have helped me to focus on the good parts of life and use the challenging parts as a reason to grow and celebrate.

The search for happiness is a journey of discovery that knows no end, very much like an ever-unfolding adventure. As one of the characters says: "old habits have a tendency to spring back...but the power to change is within you, you just have to exercise it like a muscle." I chose to show this journey being taken by a small cat named Mystic, in order to provide a fun and engaging introduction to what can amount to some pretty powerful concepts. I felt that a story about some cats, giraffes, a monkey and an elephant, would eliminate any mental interference that could arise from our preconceived human assumptions, which would in turn cultivate a deeper appreciation for the messages revealed over the course of Mystic's journey.

This book can be used both as a fun tale about a bunch of adorable animals (and a few not-so-adorable ones), as well as a roadmap to help you successfully discover your own happiness.
And since triumphs and setbacks are natural parts of life, and of the process of learning, you are free to go on this journey toward happiness unencumbered, letting Mystic's triumphs be yours, and his setbacks be a way for you to grow without having to be the one to stumble.

Happy reading!

Anne-Claire Szubaniska

Mystic

Contents

1

Mystic

Bumpa

BREAKING AWAY

The night was dark and cool, and everybody was sound asleep. Well, almost everybody. Cats who were lucky enough to be allowed outside at night were roaming around, looking for little rodents to chase or garbage to explore—cats like Mystic, a well-groomed, gray tabby with white and black stripes and piercing blue eyes. But unlike the other cats, Mystic wasn't looking to chase anyone or spill garbage all over the place. He was sitting and looking up at the stars with his friend, an elephant named Bumpa.

Nights like tonight were their favorite. It was August, and the new moon made the sky as clear as crystal. It seemed millions of stars covered the world like a blanket.

A shooting star flickered across the sky.

"Wow!" Bumpa said, bouncing heavily on the wooden platform he loved to sit on with Mystic beside him. "Did you see that? How long the tail was?"

"Yes, yes, yes, I saw it," Mystic said. "But stop jumping like that. You're going to break your board again, and your caretaker might not repair it this time. Then we'll have nothing to relax on."

Bumpa was completely undeterred by Mystic's irritation. "I know, but did you see the size of its tail?"

"Yes, it was impressive. Did you make a wish?"

1

"You bet I did!" Bumpa swished his tail from side to side. "I was saving my best wish for this one, and I made it!" He bounced on the platform again, and Mystic looked at him disapprovingly.

"Oops, sorry," laughed Bumpa, sitting still.

Mystic smiled. Bumpa wasn't trying to annoy him on purpose; he was just full of joyful energy and needed to express it, like a child at Christmas. It was actually what he loved most about Bumpa. His personality was contagious.

But even still, from time to time, Bumpa said something that annoyed Mystic. Right now, he was fixated on what Bumpa had said about his wish.

"Why haven't you ever told me about your special wish? It feels strange that you didn't share it with me. You know everything about me, and I *thought* I knew everything about you, too. Apparently I'm—"

But he didn't get a chance to finish. Bumpa burst out laughing again. "This is so typical of you," he said. "You take everything so personally, as if I like you less because I didn't tell you about *one* of my many wishes."

Even though it was the truth, Mystic was still upset by Bumpa's remark. But it wasn't just the remark. It was that Mystic knew he was too thin-skinned but didn't know how to be anything else, and that hurt. Then his hurt turned into anger.

"Why are you hurting my feelings? You know it stings me when you say things like that."

"Mystic, please." Bumpa smiled kindly. "You know I would never do anything to hurt you. Never. You get hurt, that's all."

2

Mystic pouted. He had hoped Bumpa would at least admit what he had done, but instead he kept going.

"It's the way *you* interpret things that causes you pain, not what *I* did or said."

"So why didn't you tell me about this dream of yours then?" whined Mystic. "Am I not special enough for you to share it with?"

"It has nothing to do with your worthiness, Mystic," Bumpa said tenderly. "I didn't tell you, because for a wish to come true it needs to stay in your head. It's a secret thing. I promise, though, when it comes true, I'll tell you all about it. Which I cannot wait to do!" He became animated again, dancing around on the bench.

"Do you promise that I'll be the first one you tell?"

"I promise!" Bumpa held out his foot for a high-five.

Mystic, reassured by Bumpa's promise, lifted his tiny paw and slapped it against Bumpa's. "High-five!" they shouted.

Mystic looked back up at the sky, the unpleasantness melting slowly out of him, as another shooting star etched its way across the night like a fast-moving lightning bug. He tried to think of a wish he could attach to the star and send out into the universe with it. But nothing came to him. That didn't matter much, though. He doubted that wishing on a star would result in anything real.

Bumpa is happy and free and has no trouble thinking of wishes. He just looks at the stars with complete delight, and they come to him easily. Mystic admired Bumpa so much for his free spirit. A small part of him wished he could be the same. Even if he received Bumpa's energy, felt freer and happier than usual when they were together, it seemed unfair that he couldn't be more joyful on his own.

-2-

Mystic had his ritual. He visited Bumpa both at night and at lunchtime. At around noon, he traveled from his home to the park where Bumpa lived. Over the months, the caretakers had come to expect Mystic, and when word got out that a house cat was coming to see an elephant every day, the children started coming in droves to see them.

Bumpa's beaming face reflected how the smiling crowd gathered around the edge of his enclosure gave him tremendous joy and energy. Mystic wished he could be as happy as Bumpa always seemed to be; he felt the same excitement from the crowd as Bumpa did, but he knew he wasn't as joyful and enthusiastic.

Each time he arrived, Mystic rubbed against Bumpa's huge gray feet to say hello. Bumpa then sat, enveloped Mystic in his trunk, lifted him in the air, and deposited him on his shoulder. It was always that moment at which the children bounced on their feet and let out cries of surprise, which made Bumpa smile. But to Mystic, the cries were often too piercing causing him to cringe.

It was the morning after they had watched the stars together, and Bumpa had just put Mystic on his shoulder. All the children were jumping and screaming with excitement.

"They make me so happy," Bumpa said. "I love it!"

"There must be a thousand of them today!" Mystic shouted over the din. He couldn't believe the number of

4

small faces staring down at them—he'd never seen so many at one time, and for once he felt as excited as Bumpa looked. It was a new experience, this level of joy. He liked it. "So what do you want to do today?" he asked when the overwhelming feeling had eased a little.

"Play!" Bumpa exclaimed, jumping up and down in place.

"Of course play," Mystic laughed. "We always play, don't we?" It was exactly what he loved to share with Bumpa—the crazy excitement and enthusiasm that made him almost forget that anything else in the world mattered. Without warning, Mystic jumped off Bumpa's shoulder and shouted, "Try to catch me!"

Bumpa turned instinctively to snatch Mystic out of the air with his trunk but missed, and Mystic landed lightly on his feet before him. He ran, and Bumpa chased him until Mystic darted between his legs. Bumpa rounded his back, pushed his head through his legs and stretched his trunk back toward Mystic. It was a pose both funny and perilous. The children screamed with fear, clearly thinking Bumpa might fall on himself or on Mystic, but he never did. It was all a trick, and he was able to control his motion much more easily than it seemed. They also screamed whenever Bumpa was close to catching Mystic in his trunk, but that was part of their play, too. Mystic and Bumpa would exchange a conspiratorial wink and keep going.

When both were finally exhausted, Mystic allowed Bumpa to catch him and toss him in the air. The kids shrieked at the top of their lungs as Mystic spun and twirled, but Bumpa always caught him and set him down gently at his feet.

Then they sat side-by-side, Mystic's head resting comfortably against Bumpa's warm, welcoming body. In that moment, life was perfection, and Mystic felt as though he could stay that way forever. On one side of him were the squealing, adoring children, on the other his friend. Life was good.

Too bad this cannot last for me like it does for Bumpa, Mystic thought with regret. He already felt his state of great happiness dissipating. *I wish I were as lucky as he is.*

-3-

When Mystic wasn't in the park with Bumpa, he was at home with his loving family: Jean, Pete, and their daughter Sarah. Mystic loved them all, but he loved Sarah the most.

She was not yet six years old and already looked strikingly similar to her mother: both had dense yet smooth black hair, intense brown eyes, and skin pale like cream. Also, like her mother, Sarah was sweet and kind with a gentle disposition. Whenever she played with Mystic, she was careful not to play too roughly.

The love he shared with Sarah wasn't the same as the love he shared with Bumpa, but it was equally strong. With Bumpa he could communicate directly; with Sarah it was more instinctual. She always seemed to know what he was trying to say through his body language, and Mystic could *almost* always tell what Sarah was trying to say with hers. For a human and a cat, they were well-connected. He knew other cats who didn't share *any* bond with their humans or even the other animals they interacted with daily, so he knew what they had was special.

In the early morning, Mystic slipped in through the cat door in the bottom of the kitchen door as he always did after spending his night with Bumpa. He made sure to make more noise than necessary so Sarah would hear him. Her ears were well attuned to the sounds of the cat door, and one of Mystic's greatest pleasures in life, aside from spending time with Bumpa, was when Sarah clutched him to her chest and covered his head with kisses when he came home in the morning. He felt welcome and accepted.

Sarah was sitting at the breakfast table as Mystic came in, and the second she saw him, she abandoned her cereal and ran for the door.

"You're back!" she screamed with joy, picking him up off the floor and holding him to her. Jean and Pete, who were still at the table, smiled from ear to ear and continued their breakfast. After kisses and petting, Sarah set Mystic back on the floor, and he twined himself around her legs, purring as loudly as he could. It always made Sarah giggle.

"He sounds like a motorboat."

"Sarah, come finish your breakfast," Jean said, smiling. "You're going to be late for school. And besides, Mystic has some sleep to catch up on."

"Okay." Sarah reached down to pet Mystic one final time, then reluctantly marched over to the table to finish eating while Mystic made his way upstairs to her bed.

7

As he walked, he thought about how lucky he was that he had both Sarah and Bumpa to share with. That's why he always tried to show how appreciative he was. When Sarah got home from school in the afternoon, Mystic would be asleep at the foot of her bed, recuperating from entertaining the kids with Bumpa. Sarah always anticipated it, and even before going to play with her friends next-door, she ran upstairs to play with Mystic. He also made sure he was there in the evening to spend the time between dinner and bedtime with her. When Sarah was in bed, he lay at her feet, but his favorite was when he fell asleep on her pillow beside her. Sarah would let go of her teddy bear and pull Mystic to her instead.

Once in Sarah's arms, he felt like the world had stopped turning and this moment of peace and perfection could last forever. But Bumpa would be waiting for him to star-gaze, so once she was sound asleep, Mystic snuck out again, this time taking great pains to make sure the cat door made no sound.

But all of that was for later. Now, curled up like a comma on the end of Sarah's unmade bed, Mystic drifted off to sleep, thinking about the kids he would soon entertain with Bumpa. He dreamed of being as happy as his friend, again.

-5-

"Bumpa! Hey, Bumpa!" Mystic was walking through the tunnel that connected the path to Bumpa's enclosure, calling out to him as he did every day at lunchtime. The tunnel was dark and cool, just the right size for him. Sometimes, when it was too warm outside or he hadn't gotten enough sleep in the morning, Mystic would lie down and take a nap in the cool damp beneath the rocks that made up its roof. But today he was rested and energized.

Bumpa didn't answer. From time to time, when the kids were really riled up, their screams covered Mystic's voice and Bumpa wouldn't hear him, but today everything was silent. Much more silent than it should be. He had a strange sinking feeling in his stomach and started to move more quickly.

Maybe he's asleep, Mystic thought, but something about that didn't seem right either. Bumpa was *never* asleep when Mystic was due to arrive. His heart fluttered like a sparrow trapped in a chimney. He didn't know why, but something deep inside was telling him that something horrible had happened. No matter how hard he tried to push that thought away, it remained. He started to run.

Mystic shot out of the end of the tunnel much faster than usual, and instead of seeing the enclosure he was used to—a place he had come to know as well as his own home—he emerged into a foreign landscape. The toys were gone and so were the blankets and Bumpa's bedding. His food area was empty, too. Normally, it was scattered with the remainder of Bumpa's hay and the leftover fruit he didn't enjoy, but now it had been scrubbed clean. It smelled the way the house did when Jean or Pete tidied up.

He looked up to the rim of the enclosure, expecting to see the smiling faces of the children staring down, but that was empty, too. It was strange not seeing anyone there. Mystic had never seen it totally empty during the day.

Why did they clean his pen? he wondered. It didn't make any sense at all. In all the months he had been visiting Bumpa, they'd never scrubbed it as clean as this. The sinking feeling in his stomach worsened.

Then an idea struck him: *Maybe they moved him to another pen!* It made a certain kind of sense. If they were going to clean his enclosure as thoroughly as this, they wouldn't be able to do it with Bumpa inside. They *must* have moved him.

"I just have to find where!" His shout echoed in the emptiness and came back to his ears. He heard the hope in his voice and felt comforted by it. *That has to be it,* he thought. "I'll go around the park and look in every single pen. I bet I'll find him in no time!"

Excited, he ran back through the tunnel, leaving the large empty enclosure behind. It would take a while to search the entire park, and he wanted to start as soon as possible. He ran the length of the tunnel faster than he ever had before, came out the other side, and immediately froze.

He had forgotten it was the middle of the day and the park was full of people walking around, not watching where they were going. Not to mention all the children running around, stuffed full of excitement and sugar. It could be dangerous for a little cat like him. His hope began to fade. He couldn't search now, not easily, but he didn't want to wait. Every moment he didn't know where Bumpa was, negative thoughts grew more and more vibrant, the feeling of hopelessness in his stomach more unbearable.

His chest was tense, and he was having trouble breathing. It was too much all at once—the fear of the

10

unknown, anticipation of what would come next, and perhaps worst of all, his increasing anxiety that he would never see Bumpa again.

This isn't getting me anywhere, he thought. He was still frozen on the path, people all around. Sooner or later someone would notice him. *But where should I check first?*

And then it came to him. The largest empty enclosure was the one where the polar bears used to live. It had been empty for a year, and the rumor was that they had been relocated to a place where they could be freer. He'd heard that they were happy now. He hadn't known the bears personally, but he knew the way, and it wasn't far.

He started moving, slowly at first, trying to avoid the forest of legs around him, but before long he started to run. As he ran, he became more and more certain that Bumpa would be there, that he *had* to be there. Soon he would be laughing at how worried he had been. He could see no other option.

But even before he could look into the polar bear enclosure, his hope was dashed. The Plexiglas surrounding it was cloudy.

Maybe they just haven't had time to clean it yet, he thought, grasping at whatever hope he could, but when he ran up to the dirty Plexiglas and looked down, his hope vanished. The blue paint on the bottom of the empty pool was cracked and peeling. It was obvious that no one had lived there for a long time.

The pain hit him all at once, and it was like being struck by lightning. *He's gone,* Mystic thought. *Gone forever, like the bears.* In that moment, he was certain he would never see

11

his friend again, and along with the pain came anger.

"No!" he shouted. "No, no, no! Please come back, Bumpa! I don't care if the polar bears are happier where they are now, I don't want you there! I want you here! Come back!"

His voice echoed off the empty walls of the enclosure, but there was no other sound. Bumpa didn't call back.

He felt alone, as if his world were collapsing around him.

He sat, sad and angry, for a while before deciding to move on and check the other large enclosures. He no longer had hope that he would find Bumpa in any of them—they were all being lived in by the elk, giraffes, moose, and all the other gigantic animals—but he had to go anyway. He had to be sure.

More and more people were arriving every minute, and everything felt more dangerous. He had to check, though, and so started off, moving quickly and quietly, sticking to the shadows as much as possible.

Bumpa was nowhere to be found.

Sad, dejected, and angry, Mystic decided to go home. There was nothing else for him here now.

-6-

Mystic was lost deep in his thoughts, and they were all about Bumpa. He usually enjoyed his walk home. In the stretch between the park and his house, birds were all over the place, happily flitting from branch to branch, and it normally gave him such joy to watch them. They were free, healthy, and fast—not the sort of bird he would dare chase.

12

Today, he felt more like the birds he would sometimes catch—old and sick. It was seeing the healthy birds that made him feel this way; watching them fly so freely, chattering to one another without a care in the world, made him even more aware of Bumpa's absence and how lonely he felt. He wished he could be up there with them, all his cares and worries left far below.

But that would never happen, *especially* not this morning. He walked robotically, head down, staring at the ground instead of the birds, just creeping along, dragging his lifeless tail behind him. Before he knew it, he was pulling himself through the cat door, grateful that Sarah wasn't home to see him like this. It was impossible for him to fake being happy as Pete and Jean could.

He remembered once seeing Pete come home yelling at someone on his phone in the front yard, but by the time he entered the house he was acting happy again and even laughing. Mystic had figured out that Pete had hidden his feelings to protect Sarah, but it wasn't something Mystic could do. He felt the way he felt, and there was no hiding it.

He slunk through the kitchen and upstairs to Sarah's room. He wanted nothing else in life at that moment other than to curl up at the end of her bed, and when he entered her room, he felt immediately comforted. The presence of Sarah's scent was almost as good as her hugging him. It couldn't fill the emptiness he felt inside, but it did lessen it. Maybe more than that. Mystic felt the calmest he had since discovering Bumpa was gone. He jumped up onto the bed, pressed his nose into Sarah's blanket, and curled his paw around his face. The smell of home was wonderful. He lay that way, enjoying the feeling of his sadness and pain seeping out of him. Before he knew it, he had fallen asleep.

-7-

The bang of the kitchen door closing woke him a little later. He stretched, yawned, and jumped down off the bed, his morning momentarily forgotten. Voices came up from below. It was Pete and Sarah. He ran downstairs to greet them. When he entered, they were unloading groceries onto the kitchen counter. He immediately spied a can of his favorite food. Pete was talking to Sarah, but Mystic ignored it. He could rarely tell what the humans were saying anyway. All his attention was focused on the can of food on the counter. He stretched up against the cupboard door and meowed lightly.

"He's going to need extra cuddling now, Sarah," Pete said as he took a dish from the cupboard and emptied the food into it.

"Yes, Dad, I know."

Mystic stared intensely at the dish of food in Pete's hand. It was almost to the floor, and he decided that it was close enough. He ran over and started to eat, taking large bites and gulping them down.

"Well, at least he's not too sad to eat." Pete smiled as he set Mystic's dish on the floor.

Sarah jumped up and down excitedly, then bent over and petted him for a few moments. "He loves it!"

Pete called her away. "Let him eat in peace for now. Why don't you go clean up your room?"

14

They left and Mystic was alone. As he licked the last few drops of juice from the bottom of the dish, his stomach full and his mind at ease, he thought, *I should tell Bumpa about my treat!*

Then he remembered.

It hit him with the force of a truck, and the pain returned, driving out the good feelings he'd gotten from his food. He sat heavily in front of his empty plate and stared at it. Nothing remained now but the few greasy swirls left by his tongue and the vague smell of fish. He never would have thought it possible to feel such sadness sitting in front of a plate that smelled so wonderful, but then he never would have thought that Bumpa would leave him, either.

It's not fair, he thought, sullenly licking his paw. *Being with Sarah is supposed to be fun, but without Bumpa in my life too, it's not. I want both of them, and then I'll be happy.* He went to his water dish but, before even taking a sip, decided he didn't really want it. All he wanted right now was the only thing that could give him relief.

He heard Sarah moving around in her room, and he ran upstairs to be with her.

She was sitting on the floor in the middle of her room, playing with her hairdresser set. She waved to him with her hairbrush.

Normally, he would hop up on the bed and watch her as she played, creating an elaborate imaginary world that she immersed herself in totally. He loved her imagination and felt closer to her when he watched her play. She had the same capacity for creation he had; when she was in her world of haircuts, perms, and hair-dyeing, it was as real to her as it was when he pretended a ball of paper was a mouse or a piece of dust floating through the air was a bird. Mystic had realized early on that this was a special thing they shared. He had never seen Jean and Pete imagine anything, and the few times he had tried to get them involved in Sarah's world by rubbing against their legs or meowing, they just thought he wanted food.

Today was different. Today he needed attention and didn't feel like joining Sarah in her imaginary world. He walked across the floor, rubbed against her back, and let out a little whimper.

Sarah turned at once, grabbed him under his belly, and put him across her lap. "I know, Mystic," she said, her voice full of compassion. "Daddy told me about your friend—that he was taken away. I'm so sorry."

Mystic was shocked. He had never been able to translate what humans were saying—there were so many words, and none of them made sense to him—though he could read their emotions and body language quite well. But now he understood. Not her words, necessarily, but he knew Sarah understood he had lost his friend.

He faced her. "Where is Bumpa? What happened to him? Is he coming back?" The questions were out of his mouth before he realized it, and after they were, he felt a little foolish. He knew Sarah couldn't understand him, that all she would hear was meowing.

"I know you're sad, Mystic. But I love you, and I'll always be here for you. You're not alone, you know?" She hugged him to her tightly, more tightly than usual, and planted a kiss on his head. She held him that way for a little while, until she became antsy to dive back into her imaginary world and set him on the bed.

Soon after, Sarah was so lost inside her play, talking to her imaginary clients about what color they were looking to dye their hair and how much they wanted cut off, that she didn't even notice when Mystic hopped down off the bed, went down the stairs, and out the cat door.

-*8*-

Mystic sauntered down the street until he was in front of the biggest house in the neighborhood where his friend Ulysses lived. Ulysses was a pure white cat with delicate features and silky fur. He looked so refined and distinguished that you wouldn't know his home life was chaotic. He lived with three boys between the ages of two to ten and their parents, and something was always happening in their home.

Ulysses had once told Mystic that, when everyone in the house was a little tense or on edge, he only had to rub himself against them for the mood to settle. Sometimes, though, not even that was enough and someone would kick him away in irritation. He never minded, because whenever that happened, someone would immediately come to his defense, screaming at whoever had kicked him, and scoop him into their arms to protect him.

It never stayed like that for long, though, and the calm would always return. Mystic knew that calm for Ulysses' family would be chaotic for Jean, Pete, Sarah, but Ulysses seemed to enjoy his life very much despite that. More than

17

that, he seemed to thrive in it.

Mystic had often thought he was very lucky not to have Ulysses' life; he could not have stood such a high level of energy all the time—he was far too peaceful for that. Now, he felt differently. If he had been too busy at home with his family, he wouldn't have had time to go to the park and meet Bumpa in the first place, and he wouldn't be feeling this horrible now.

"Hey, Mystic," Ulysses called from along the sidewalk as Mystic approached. "What's up?"

"Nothing good," Mystic said with a voice as heavy and full of pain as he felt inside.

"Uh-oh," Ulysses said lightly. Mystic had known Ulysses for more than a year now, and Ulysses had accused him in the past of being overly sensitive. His light attitude got on Mystic's nerves sometimes, but he couldn't tell Ulysses that, or he would level the same accusation at him again.

He remembered the last time he had been depressed and had come across Ulysses.

"What's wrong, Mystic?" he had asked.

"My human, Sarah, has been ignoring me lately," Mystic had replied. "She's spending so much more time with her friends than she is with me. She hasn't even picked me up today."

Ulysses had laughed. "I've never seen a cat who acts so much like a human. Normally, cats are just happy with themselves and don't need anything or anyone else to feel good. They love interacting with others, but it's not *necessary* to make them happy. But you seem so dependent on attention to feel good!"

Mystic had said nothing but started to pout.

"Just because Sarah is spending time with other people doesn't mean she doesn't love you anymore."

Mystic hadn't been convinced.

That had been the same day he'd met Bumpa for the first time, and that evening when he had passed by Ulysses' house on the way home, walking lightly and happily, Ulysses had asked him what had changed. Mystic had told him about Bumpa and the incredible day they had spent together in the park.

"You see!" Ulysses had exclaimed. "If Sarah was around as much as she used to be, you never would have gone to the park, had an amazing day, and made a new friend!" Mystic had agreed that the day had gone perfectly.

"And do you love Sarah any less now that you've made a new friend?" Ulysses had asked a little sarcastically, but it was playful not mean.

"No, of course not... I can love more than one friend at a time."

"So, can Sarah."

Mystic had recognized that Ulysses was right, but it didn't make it easy to accept. The next time Sarah had spent more time with her friends and had played with him less, he'd still felt abandoned. He had also been hurt when Bumpa had told him about playing with his caretakers and receiving treats for doing so. Mystic didn't like feeling excluded.

And now, watching Ulysses as he spoke, Mystic could tell that the white cat assumed it was the same old thing bothering him and wasn't taking him seriously. Mystic grew more disheartened. If he couldn't even talk to Ulysses about it, who could he talk to?

"So, what is it this time, Mystic?" Ulysses asked.

"Not that you care, but Bumpa is gone." Mystic sank to the ground under the weight of his words.

Ulysses' mouth dropped open in surprise. "Mystic, of course I care! That's awful! What happened to him? Was he sick, or did he have an accident?"

"He's not gone *that* way," Mystic sighed. "He's just gone...He's not in his pen."

"Oh! Is that all?"

Mystic heard the relief in Ulysses' voice. "What do you mean is that all? Isn't it enough? Do you think I should be relieved that I can't find my best friend?"

"No, but it's better than if something had happened to him, isn't it? He's still alive, isn't he?"

"Yes, yes, of course." Logically, Mystic knew Ulysses was right, but logic and emotion were two different things. Emotionally, Mystic couldn't help the way he felt, even though he knew it was selfish. "But if something like that *had* happened, at least I'd know where he was."

"You don't mean that." Ulysses was suddenly sterner than Mystic had ever heard him, and it shocked him a little. "You're just angry, and it's okay to be angry, but I know you would never wish anything bad to happen to one of your friends, even if it made you feel better in some way. Would you?"

"No, I don't wish anything bad had happened," Mystic said, his voice soft and deflated. "But I don't know what to do."

"Have you tried asking the other animals at the park?"

"It was too busy when I was there, too many people…it was too dangerous to be running around."

"Then why don't you stay here with me until the sun reaches the other side of the trees?" Ulysses said. "That's when the park closes to the children and you can talk to the animals without being afraid. I'll even come with you if you want."

Mystic didn't want to wait—he wanted his answer now—but Ulysses was right. It was smarter to go a little later when they would have an easier time. He realized that he was lucky to have a friend like Ulysses, even if he didn't always seem to care about Mystic's problems. He cared now, and Mystic was no longer alone in his search.

-9-

By the time the sun had traveled to the other side of the trees in Ulysses' yard, Mystic and Ulysses had formed a plan and divided up the animals they would talk to, cutting their work in half.

Ulysses would speak to the exotic birds, farm animals, lions, and the pigeons who hung around the park eating the other animal's leftovers. Mystic, on the other hand, would talk to the tigers, zebras, seals, and then finish with the giraffes.

It took just over an hour to speak to everyone except the giraffes, and with every animal he walked away from without an answer, Mystic became more and more dismayed. He noticed that, the more upset he became, the

21

more compassionate the other animals became, until he wasn't really feeling upset anymore. He continued to act upset because the attention was nice… more than that—he loved it.

By the time he reached Lili and Lulu's, he no longer even hoped the giraffes would know where Bumpa was. But at least he would get more compassion and attention, and that was enough to keep him going.

When he approached their enclosure, Lulu and Lili raised their heads from their dish of pellets and acacia branches. The railing surrounding the pit they lived in was the same height as their heads, and Mystic crawled up under it close to them.

"Hi, Lulu and Lili," he said, his voice low and sad. "I'm here because—"

"Because you're looking for Bumpa," Lili said.

Mystic froze for a moment, not expecting to hear Bumpa's name, and in that instant all the hope he had set out with suddenly returned. "Yes!" he exclaimed, unable to help it, a thousand questions at the tip of his tongue. But before he could ask, Lili cut him off.

"We're sorry, Mystic," she said, shaking her head, staring at him with her big blue eyes. "We don't know where Bumpa is. We saw his caretaker come first thing this morning and take him away in the big truck."

"And I know the truck," Lulu interrupted. "It's the same one that took Snowy and Icy away."

"The polar bears," Lili added.

"The humans said they were going somewhere called a bear sanctuary, but I doubt they took Bumpa there," Lulu said.

Mystic's face crumpled, all the hope that had returned for such a brief moment already scattered to the wind. Snowy and Icy had been taken away and had never come back. *Bumpa's never coming back,* Mystic thought. Flashes of happy moments shared with Bumpa crossed his mind and intensified his sense of loss. But suddenly, the memory of the other night lashed his heart. Bumpa had sent his greatest wish to the sky, and now he was gone.

Was that his secret wish? To leave? But he promised me that he would tell me!

Betrayal and hurt bubbled up within him, replacing hope. He felt more alone than ever. Negative thoughts swirled through his mind like a cloud of flies, blotting out everything else. Mystic wanted to open his mouth and just scream. It felt like the whole world was against him.

This is unfair! How could Bumpa leave me behind like this? How could he be so selfish??

He might have gone on thinking those negative, hurtful thoughts for a long time, if he hadn't been interrupted by Ulysses running up and stopping beside him out of breath.

"Why did you come running up like that?" Mystic asked, but he wasn't really interested in the answer. His hope of finding Bumpa was completely gone, and nothing else really mattered.

"I talked with the pigeons," Ulysses said. "They told me all about a big truck and the elephant going inside, and I thought you'd want to know."

Mystic's ears perked up. "They said Bumpa *went* into the truck?" he asked, curious again. "Like *going* in on his own?"

23

"Yes! They even said he looked happy and jumped up and down inside."

Mystic thought back to when Bumpa jumped up and down on his platform. He could easily picture his friend doing that in the back of the truck, and if he hadn't been so sad and hurt, it would have been funny.

"So that *was* his wish," he said under his breath. He was looking at Lulu and Lili, but he wasn't really seeing them. Stuck in his own mind, all Mystic could see was Bumpa staring up at the stars and making the wish that would take him away forever. "But why? Why did he want to leave me? Why did he want to hurt me like that?" No one answered. "Well, at least now I know why he didn't tell me his wish…because he knew I would have begged him to stay here with me."

All was silent for a few minutes but for the crickets and the faraway roar of traffic. Finally, Ulysses spoke up, his voice measured and cautious.

"Mystic, why do you say that Bumpa wanted to leave *you*? Don't you think he wanted to leave this place, his pen, and not you?"

"Maybe, but I live here, don't I?" Mystic shouted. "I belong here, and he belongs here with me! But he left, and that means he wanted to leave me, too! He didn't even tell me about it, he kept it a secret. I feel so betrayed!"

"Or maybe he kept it a secret so you two could enjoy every single moment together right up to the end," Lulu said softly.

"If you had known he was leaving, you wouldn't have enjoyed any of your time together, would you?" Lili added.

24

"Instead, you would have been sad and depressed. You wouldn't even have the great memories you do."

Lulu was behind her, nodding as she spoke.

"Are you all on Bumpa's side?" Mystic shouted angrily.

"There are no sides, Mystic," Ulysses said.

Mystic didn't even hear him. Blood was rushing through his ears, and he felt the anger as heat in his face. Instead of trying to talk sense into the giraffes or Ulysses, Mystic turned and stomped toward home. He wanted to be alone now.

Mystic heard Ulysses' fast steps chasing after him.

"Go away, Ulysses. I'll be fine," he said before the white cat got too close. "I'm going home, and you should, too. There's nothing more we can do."

"I'm with you, Mystic," Ulysses said a little out of breath. "I just think you're not seeing things straight. Bumpa would never do anything to hurt you, and you know that. He just needed to take care of himself, to do what was best for him."

Mystic kept walking, keeping up a brisk pace but not quite running, and pretended not to hear anything Ulysses was saying.

"Besides, I'm sure Bumpa had a good reason to keep it a secret," Ulysses continued. "Bumpa always did what he could to protect you, not hurt you, and I know you know that too."

Mystic stopped and faced Ulysses. "I know," he said finally, letting his anger melt away a little. "I know everything you're saying is true, but I can't help the way I feel. I'm upset right now, and I don't know how to feel anything else."

2

Freedom

A NEW FRIEND

Ulysses returned home, and Mystic continued walking down the path toward his own, when he suddenly stopped. The thought of being around Sarah and his human family didn't fill him with the joy and happiness it usually did. It would be a chore to try and be a friend to Sarah tonight.

He knew of a safe place in the park where some of the wild cats lived, where he could spend a night or two. The cats always treated him well and were friendly even though they had no human families of their own. Sometimes they would even share some food with him, and they were always captivated by his stories.

Mystic headed back to the park, content with the idea of sharing his grief and a nice meal. It was dusk now, and the woman who sometimes brought food to the wild cats did so only after dark, so he hadn't yet missed it. And after that, he would have some time to himself to figure out what to do next.

The wild cats greeted him with their usual enthusiasm and friendliness, but this time it was short-lived. Mystic's story wasn't a happy or silly one about something Sarah, Jean, or Pete had done. This time the story was sad. He told them in detail what had happened to him since this morning when he discovered Bumpa's empty enclosure, and the cats hung on his every word. Mystic felt the same as he had this afternoon going from animal to animal, telling his sad story, and before too long he forgot again that he was sad. He was fully absorbed by his tale of woe. He went into great detail (it took him even longer to tell the story than it had that afternoon), painting a vivid picture of his sadness, helplessness, and betrayal. With great vigor, he told of his anger at Bumpa, at Lili and Lulu and Ulysses, everyone who was against him, and then wrapped up his story by asking what he had done to deserve such treatment. It was an amazing performance.

"I really don't know what to do," he finished. He thought that maybe one of the wild cats would have a solution to his problem, a magical formula he could follow that would somehow fix everything, but the response was not what he expected.

"Why don't you stay with us?" Dusty asked cheerfully from the back of the crowd. Dusty had been a white fluffy cat, but now her fur was so full of dust and dirt that she was a dingy gray.

"Yes, why don't you?" all the cats chimed in at different times, creating a chorus of voices. There was excitement in the crowd at the thought of Mystic staying with them, but he was becoming annoyed again. He was deeply disappointed. He wanted ideas of how to find Bumpa, *smart* ideas, not selfish solutions.

All they think about is themselves! They don't care about my sadness or my pain. They only think about themselves and how much fun they can have with me here.

The other cats were still excited, chatting back and forth

with one another, and none noticed that Mystic was getting angry.

Everyone is so selfish, he thought furiously.

He was so totally absorbed by his anger and disappointment that he had failed to notice a black cat near the back of the crowd. Her fur was so dark and glossy it was almost blue and shone. But unlike the other cats, she didn't seem moved by Mystic's tale of misery. In fact, as she listened to his story, she was smiling slightly from her place at the back of the crowd. Her tail flicked slowly back and forth as if that was soothing, and her green eyes were half closed. Her entire body rocked in time with her tail, and she looked at peace, almost as though in a state of meditation.

That was how Mystic had first spied her. It had felt as though someone in the group was staring directly at him. He looked up over the heads of the other cats and saw her at the back, slightly separated from the others, a look of bliss on her face. When their eyes met, her knowing smile changed into a wide and beautiful one. Mystic found himself struck by a sudden shyness. He didn't dare move or say anything.

There was something astoundingly beautiful about her. A strong presence emanated from her, traveling through the crowd of wild cats toward Mystic, who even from this distance could feel the power of her presence. He could only stare at her and felt lucky to do so. There was something important happening here—Mystic could feel it all throughout his body—but he couldn't yet say exactly what.

The black cat stood with slow elegance and walked through the crowd toward Mystic. The wild cats parted before her, clearing a path without realizing they were doing so.

Mystic's heart began to thump hard against his ribs as she got closer, though he couldn't understand why. He was usually confident around females; in fact, he couldn't remember the last time he had been nervous.

Why am I feeling like this?

The black cat walked up, stopped a foot in front of him, and sat down on the grass. Mystic was captivated by her vivid green eyes, and when she spoke, he watched them.

"Please, Mystic, stop waiting for others to help you." Her voice was soft, melodious and carried a feeling of calm. "Only you can help yourself."

"But why?" Mystic said.

The black cat spoke gently. "Because seeking help from the outside requires you to feel good on the inside first. It's the only way you'll be open to it." The knowing smile returned to her face and she looked satisfied, as if she had just accomplished something very important.

Although still entranced by the black cat's presence, Mystic felt the old anger starting to creep back. "It's like a riddle," he said, annoyed. *Who is she to tell me just to feel good?* he thought. *I've just lost my best friend in the whole world, and she says 'feel good' like it's that simple! And why does she want to help me anyway? Is she crazy or what?* He wanted to scream all of this at her and more, but instead he sat speechless. Her confidence was evident both in the way she sat—comfortably, undisturbed by what was going on around her—and in the way she spoke. It had been Mystic's experience that, whenever someone wanted to get a point across, they would talk and talk and never let you get a word

30

in edgewise. But this black cat said what she had to say and then stopped talking, giving him time to process the information and respond.

It was a little disturbing, and it was that more than anything else that finally caused him to shout, "Who do you think you are telling me just to *feel good, feel good?* Haven't you noticed that I'm sad and angry for a reason—a reason I can't control?"

"If you practiced feeling joyful the way you practice finding excuses to not be happy, you would always feel *amazing,* no matter what happened to you," she said, almost as though oblivious to Mystic's irritation. As if it didn't matter to her one bit. She smiled again. "It may seem simple, but this is the key to figuring out how to be reunited with your friend, Mystic. In the end it's your call, but you really should focus on feeling good no matter what." She stopped talking, licked her paw, and cleaned her ears with it, completely at ease despite Mystic's growing annoyance.

But in spite of that, and in spite of not being able to bear hearing what the black cat was saying, Mystic felt the kindness and warmth behind her words. He knew she thought she was helping, but to him it wasn't helpful. It was nasty. Finally, it became too much.

"Don't you think I'm suffering enough?" he yelled. "You want me to feel guilty for not feeling happy, too? And you try to put the blame on *me,* make *me* responsible for being unable to find my friend?"

Incredibly, the black cat's calm remained as did her small, knowing smile. In fact, it grew slightly larger as she spoke. "I'm not trying to make you feel worse," she said

31

kindly. "I'm pushing you a little because I trust in you. I believe in you. You can do it, Mystic—you can be happy *now*."

After his outburst, Mystic felt drained but a little better. What the black cat was saying sounded crazy, but he *wanted* it to be true. *I asked for help, and the wild cats weren't helping me at all, and then all of a sudden she showed up. Who knows, maybe she is the help I was asking for.* It still felt crazy to him, and his anger remained, but it was no longer the dominant feeling. He wanted to at least try to understand what she was talking about before deciding what to do. What could it hurt?

"This isn't a trick or a lie, Mystic, I promise you *can* be happy, and you can be reunited with your friend. I've seen it time and time again…But it's really up to you, and whether or not you want to put in the work." The black cat enunciated each word as if they were all equally important and she wanted all to reach him on a deeper level. Before he knew it, he was listening raptly, and he felt a slight glimmer of hope. "I know work can sound scary, but it's worth it, trust me. Decide that you're going to find a way to feel good, or at least feel *better*, here and now, and you'll see, after you get the hang of it, it becomes a lot of fun! Like a game! When you start to feel better, you'll begin looking for more and more reasons to feel even better than that, like you're trying to break your own record every day."

She laughed, and to Mystic she looked completely lost in her own words, as if watching a beautiful memory replaying before her eyes. The sound was as melodious as her voice, and Mystic had to work not to be distracted by it.

"And why should I feel good when everything that's happening to me and around me should be making me *really* sad and angry?"

The black cat's expression blossomed, turning her from elegant to dazzling, lit by a life that had been there the whole time but below the surface. "Because once you start feeling good inside, *truly* feeling good, then your questions will be answered."

"But—"

"Shhhh, just listen for now. Just decide to trust and try to feel better. What do you have to lose in trying?"

"I'm scared that others won't give me any consideration," he answered sincerely. "The sadder I am, the more others are compassionate. It feels good. I feel important. If I'm too happy, they'll think I don't need them and I'll be alone." He sighed. "I can't lose anything more today, not after losing Bumpa." Mystic had expected the black cat to respond with compassion, but instead she burst out laughing. His annoyance flared up again.

"Oh, Mystic…don't you realize what you just said?" she asked. "Is *that* why you're always looking for a reason to be unhappy? Because you want to be pitied and through that get others' attention?" She laughed again.

With that, she had done it, and Mystic was truly angry once more. He opened his mouth to scream at her, to scream all the things he was thinking and hadn't dared say before. But before he could, the black cat gracefully leapt beside him and placed her right paw gently over his mouth.

"Shhhh," she whispered. "Just find a way to be happy and watch what happens. Trust in it, and trust in me, too."

She looked at him with a kindness he had never experienced, and when she removed her paw from his mouth, all his angry words and accusations were gone. He wanted to stay forever in this sensation of love, the same way he wanted to stay forever in Sarah's arms.

But like everything else today, the moment ended. The black cat smiled at him, turned her back, and leapt away into the crowd. In a heartbeat, she was gone.

Mystic stood motionless, breathing in the feeling of love the black cat had left in her wake. But that too faded and was gone before too long, replaced by a wave of loneliness worse than he had experienced before. He felt as though he'd lost two friends that day.

It was at that moment he realized he didn't even know her name.

-2-

Mystic turned back to the crowd. He no longer felt angry or annoyed. In fact, he felt nothing. He was empty inside, and he was tired.

He told the cats that he didn't feel like talking anymore and asked if he could stay a night with them. They seemed thrilled to say yes. After they led him to a nice old tree on the outskirts of their territory, he rolled himself against the ground at its base and fell asleep almost at once.

Sometime later, he felt a light pawing at his face and opened his eyes to see an old orange angora cat. Mystic knew him as Tiger, one of the wild cats from the park. He was nudging Mystic gently. It was fully dark now, and the chirping crickets were loud.

"The human woman who brings us food has come," Tiger said. "She also brought some milk with her this time. Come and have some before it's all gone."

Mystic stood up, still half asleep, his stomach churning with hunger. He thought back to the last time he had eaten and remembered it had been when Pete had given him his favorite food earlier that day. It felt like such a long time ago. As he followed Tiger to where the cats were assembled eating, he was grateful to his friends for so willingly sharing their food.

He ate quickly, not trying to talk to anyone and no one trying to talk to him. When he was done, he made his way back to his tree. His belly was full, he was satiated for the time being, and he was looking forward to falling back to sleep.

As he was stumbling across the threshold into the world of dreams, the black cat's words from earlier came back to him so loudly it was almost as if she were beside him speaking them again.

Find a way to feel good.

Once you feel good, it will become addictive, and you will start to search out ways to keep that feeling.

When you focus on feeling good and start to feel better, you'll find the answers to your questions will become clear to you.

Her words echoed in his mind as he rested at the base of the tree, the feeling of happiness and comfort growing greater, until a new voice spoke up, one he didn't recognize. It startled him out of his doze:

"When you give yourself up to happiness, it will be easy for you to achieve everything you want. Nothing will be out of reach as long as you follow your joyful intuition."

Mystic opened his eyes, surprised. The words he had just heard hadn't come from the black cat, but at the same time he knew he hadn't dreamed them—he hadn't been fully asleep. It felt very real, like a presence standing beside him had spoken. He glanced around to see if anyone was close by, but he was by himself. It was a little disturbing, but he decided not to let it bother him. He stretched, arching his back high and extending his legs in front of him as far as he could, and then curled back into a ball. He closed his eyes and brought up an image of Sarah in his mind, which made him smile.

"You're beginning to learn how to reach me, you see?"

Mystic jumped up on all fours immediately and let out a frightened squeak. He looked all around him and walked in a large circle around the tree, even peering up into the leaves, trying to see who had just spoken aloud. As far as he could tell, he was still alone.

What is happening to me? he thought, annoyed. *Am I going crazy?* It certainly felt like he was. He decided to go for a short walk down the path and back to calm down and clear his mind. He came back to the tree a few minutes later, but before closing his eyes and trying to sleep, he decided to try something.

"Please, I need sleep," he said aloud in the darkness. "I need rest; just stop talking to me." He felt foolish talking to the emptiness around him and laughed at himself, but he felt calmer than he had a moment ago. He closed his eyes.

Sleep eluded him, though. Every time he got close to drifting off, he woke, certain he would hear the voice again. But he didn't. Finally, he fell asleep and slept until late the following morning.

-3-

Mystic awoke and had a few moments of happiness until he noticed he was sleeping outside under a tree. Then everything that had happened came flooding back to him.

The pain was stronger than it had been yesterday, and he felt as though he were losing control of everything (his body, his emotions, even his mind). *Why does the pain have to be here? I was in such a good mood when I woke up. Why did the pain come back and ruin it?* The day that had begun so pleasantly had quickly turned sour. He became angry at everyone and everything again. *Why is this happening to me?* But before he could continue with his self-pity, he was startled by the black cat.

"I won't always be here to help you, Mystic," she said from behind him. Before he could turn to look at her, she leapt over him and landed before him gracefully. "You're not the only one I'm helping, you know, and I won't be able to continue with you if you don't even try."

"Try what?" Mystic asked curtly.

"Try to stop being the victim," she said. "I know it's hard to understand now, but you have the power to control your emotions. You just have to learn how to replace pain with any positive feeling you choose, then practice that all the time."

37

Control my emotions? Stop being the victim? Mystic had never felt so enraged in his entire life. He wanted to open his mouth and scream all that rage and anger out until he couldn't scream anymore, but the black cat resumed talking. Only now, her voice was louder and more powerful.

"You need to understand that what happens to you shouldn't dictate how you feel, okay? *You* decide how you react to things and how they affect your happiness, not anything or anyone else." As soon as she finished speaking, she smiled serenely and her look of peace returned.

Mystic was baffled. He didn't know how to respond. He wanted to dismiss everything this annoying cat was saying, just write her off as crazy, and ignore everything she told him. But deep down, a part of him agreed with everything she said. Even if it didn't make sense.

"Mystic, you're not just a puppet controlled by what's happening outside you, and you're definitely not a puppet to your emotions," she said. "You're extremely powerful like we all are. You can control your mental attitude and change your life and the lives of those around you. Do you understand that?"

Despite his confusion, something in what she said rang true, and Mystic nodded slowly.

"Feeling better is easy once you know how," she said. "It's all about changing what you focus on. And once you do, you'll be able to listen to your intuition. And this…." She closed her eyes and smiled in a way that made it seem as if she was having the most wonderful dream, or eating an incredibly tasty meal. "This is the most amazing feeling in the world."

Mystic didn't know what intuition was and was about to ask, but the black cat spoke before he could.

"Intuition is the part of you that recognizes me."

How did she know what I was thinking about? he wondered.

She smiled and licked her paw demurely. "It's the thing within you that makes you listen to me, and makes you feel positive about me. You're feeling it right now."

She was right. It was that deep down part of him that said he should trust the black cat even when his mind was telling him she was crazy. It was the part that recognized what she was saying was true, even though he couldn't make sense of it. It was as if that part of him was extremely intelligent, but he hadn't realized it before now, and he didn't know how to access it.

"Well, if it's that easy, then why doesn't everyone do it?" he said. "And if it's true, then why hasn't anyone ever told me how to do it before?"

The black cat smiled widely, and Mystic felt pleased with himself. It was nice that he could make her smile that way just by showing interest and asking questions.

"Because they've been told to fear the easy answer and they tell themselves exactly what you did—if it was that easy, then everyone would be doing it. And you know what?"

Mystic shook his head.

"They use that as an excuse not to try. And that's why you don't see much success…because very few will even *try* to try." She laughed at her little joke.

The sound of her laughter perked up his mood a bit more,

and he waited for her to continue. He felt as though he could listen to her speak forever. It wasn't because what she was saying made sense, not really anyway, but the sound of her voice was almost intoxicating.

"Or," she teased, "they might also be scared to try because they fear being left alone."

Mystic looked away in shame.

"It's all right, Mystic, it's nothing to be ashamed of," she said softly. "You aren't the only one who does that. The first step to changing it is realizing that you're doing it."

He relaxed a little.

"Besides, doesn't it feel so much better to have someone drawn to you because your happiness inspires them than because they pity you and want to share in your misery?" She made a face when she said the last part as if she had bitten into something sour. "That kind of attention doesn't make you feel good in the long run. It's not nourishing and it doesn't last. Sort of like eating dead bugs instead of your favorite meal."

He considered what she was saying in silence. He wanted to trust her, but then again, he'd just met her last night. He still didn't even know her name or who she was. But she wasn't telling him to do anything risky. She was only saying he needed to try to feel better each and every moment of his life. There wasn't anything dangerous in trying that. Was there?

"I know it's a lot of information to take in all at once, but you *can* change if you work at it," the black cat insisted. "Old habits have a tendency to spring back, so you'll have to be patient with yourself and not get discouraged when you think, or see, or judge things negatively. It's a part of the process. But the power to change is within you, you just need to exercise it like a muscle."

Mystic loved the idea of having power within him. When he was a younger cat, he used to imagine he had superpowers and could save his friends from all sorts of danger. Now, this black cat was telling him he did have a power. The idea was very alluring.

"What's my power? And how do I—" But the black cat placed her paw against his lips again. Mystic felt electrified from head to toe by a brief, intense wave of joy.

"Whoa, whoa, whoa, hold on there," she giggled. "Don't overthink this. It's very simple. Just repeat to yourself that all is well. Tell yourself that your friend is alive and happy wherever he is, that you're alive and in good health here, and that your human family loves you." She stopped but left her paw over Mystic's mouth. He gazed into her eyes, hypnotized. "Find all the reasons you can to trigger a feeling of wellbeing within you. And before you know it, it will happen naturally. Soon, it will be a habit. Just keep practicing."

With that, she turned and bounded away into the bushes, and he was left alone beneath the tree where he had slept, speechless.

-4-

Mystic stood there for a while, thinking about the black cat as if still hypnotized by her presence. But before too long, he came back fully to his senses and realized he was in pain once again.

The black cat's departure had left a void within him, as though she had removed some vital part when she left. She annoyed him with the things she said sometimes and her overwhelming positive attitude, but at the same time her presence made him feel more at peace—as if he needed nothing else but her in the whole world to be happier, more fulfilled.

When she was around, boredom, fear, even time itself no longer seemed to exist, and that left him puzzled. He'd never experienced these feelings before, not even with Bumpa or Sarah, and he had to admit he enjoyed them as much as he was confused by them.

He only wished that the sense of peace he had when the black cat was near remained after she left. But even as he thought about the joy she brought him, his old thoughts came back, and behind those, the old feelings of sadness.

He thought about Bumpa being gone, and with that came depression. All the expectation of power the black cat had spoken of was gone. It was that expectation that had driven him to listen to her, and try to believe her.

But I can't feel better with Bumpa gone, and I wouldn't want to, he thought angrily. *It's impossible anyway!* His pain was poignant. He felt unable to overcome it on his own.

The nerve of that black cat! I actually listened to her, and she had me believing such silly things. She didn't take my pain seriously. She even tried to make me feel guilty for feeling bad, as if it's my own fault! And that was what hurt the most. She had given him false hope, lifted him up, and when he'd fallen, it had been much further than before.

He paced around and around the tree trunk, so completely lost in his thoughts that he almost didn't see a group of people until they were just about on top of him. It was a family of four—a boy and a girl, who were laughing at a little black dog running around them in circles yapping happily, and their parents behind them. The woman's face looked the way Pete's had the time the raccoons knocked over the garbage cans and scattered trash all over the yard. The man beside her, on the other hand, looked content to watch the children playing in the warm morning air.

The dog jumped up on the little girl and licked her face, causing her to burst out laughing. The little boy laughed, too, and soon they were rolling on the ground, playing with the dog and laughing even harder. As Mystic watched them, a smile surfaced on his face. He wished he could be like them right now, playing and laughing as they were. It was almost as if he could actually share their happiness without being involved. He felt something loosen in his chest. Some of the anger that had been building since the black cat left was gone, and all because the kids had distracted him with their happiness.

Wow! he thought. *I wouldn't have believed it could happen this easily, but I'm starting to feel better!* He was so involved with watching the kids and dog that when the woman spoke, it startled him. He couldn't fully understand what she was saying, but her tone was loud and angry, her body language aggressive.

"How can you be so happy, Paul?"

"I'm not happy honey, I'm just enjoying seeing our kids so happy," the man said.

"Well, that's what I mean," the woman snapped. "How can you even enjoy anything now?"

Wow, what a pain that woman is, Mystic thought. He sensed her unwillingness to be as happy as the rest of them were but couldn't understand why.

"I know you're in pain right now, and I'm in pain too, believe me," the man said, looking away from his children. "But I want to feel better. I want to stop suffering, or at least suffer less, and you're treating me like some sort of criminal."

"It's not a crime to try to feel better," the woman said, and Mystic heard in her voice that she was resisting the urge to scream. "It hurts me that you have no consideration for *my* pain and *my* sadness, as if I don't matter to you."

"Well, that works both ways." The man sounded sarcastic now. "You could try being happier with me and the kids, instead of complaining that I'm not unhappy enough for you."

"I just can't be happy!" the woman screamed. "I just can't!"

"And because you can't feel better, won't even try to, I'm the monster, right?" The man was yelling now, too.

"You're not a monster." The woman's voice was softer and exhausted now. "You hurt me because you're happy when I'm not, and—"

Mystic was so fascinated by what was going on before him that, when another voice spoke up, he jumped. This voice wasn't from the man or the woman, and he understood what it said perfectly.

"Does she remind you of someone?"

Mystic swiveled his head from side to side and looked up into the branches of the tree but saw no one.

"Don't be afraid," the voice said. "I'm the part of you Freedom was telling you about."

"Freedom?" Mystic asked, confused for a moment, but then it came to him. "You mean the black cat?"

"Yes!" the voice shouted happily.

"But who are *you*?" Mystic was still looking around. "And where are you?"

"I'm inside you," the voice giggled. "And everywhere."

I'm going crazy, he thought with sudden certainty. *I'm crazy, and that black cat made me this way.* His heart thumped faster and faster as his fear returned. He didn't want to be crazy, but he was hearing voices, and there wasn't any other explanation for that, was there?

The voice came again, but it was much quieter now, as though it were coming from miles away. "Stop," it begged, "or I won't be able to help you. I can only come to you if you're relaxed or thinking positively."

Mystic didn't move; his fear had frozen him to the spot.

"You're losing me," the voice called from even farther away, now barely a whisper. "You're losing me..." And then it was gone.

When everything was quiet, Mystic felt he could move. All he wanted was to be as far from here as possible. The family was still a little way away, the parents arguing with one another but more quietly now. The children were still laughing and playing with the dog. Mystic looked at them longingly, took three deep breaths to help clear his mind, and started to run as fast as he could. He didn't know where he was going, but running felt good.

When Mystic reached the other side of the park, he spied a well-grown maple tree in a quiet place away from the other animals and humans. He climbed into the branches as high as he could and settled down inside a cathedral of leaves. He looked down to make sure no one had followed him. He was alone and relieved.

Once he was comfortable, he thought about the voice and what it had said. *What was that thing, and where did it come from? And why did it ask if the woman reminded me of someone? I don't know anyone as annoying as that, do I?* He thought about everyone he had encountered in the last few days, and no one came to mind. *That woman was miserable. The kids were having so much fun, and she just wanted to stay in her bad mood. Boy, what a pain! She should just learn to be hap—*

And then it hit him like a bolt of lightning out of a clear blue sky. It was *he*, Mystic, that the voice was talking about. He thought then not of everyone he had met in the last few days but of the way he had been behaving the last few days: he'd been angry at the black cat, Freedom, and the wild cats for not taking his pain seriously, angry that the wild cats were happy he was going to stay the night with them, and annoyed that they hadn't offered him a solution to his problem. He remembered going from animal to animal in the park looking for Bumpa and being happy at the pity and sympathy he received from them.

I was even mad at Bumpa for having his wish come true. Mystic felt his cheeks turn pink under his fur. "I have to change. I don't want to be like that woman in the park." And for the first time, he thought it was really possible. Remembering the children playing with their dog still brought a smile to his face as it had earlier, even when the pain had seemed insurmountable.

And it was then that what Freedom had been telling him finally clicked into place. The understanding that came from her words was total, and he felt a wave of optimism and hope. It wasn't the hope he'd had earlier when he was telling Freedom he would try simply because of the expectation of power. Now Mystic felt hope that he might be okay even if he couldn't find Bumpa—not that he would give up trying— but he finally understood the power he had. He could choose to dwell on the sadness or choose to be happier instead. It seemed incredible. He, who had always felt like a victim of his painful emotions! Before Freedom, no one had told him it was even possible to control them, let alone how to do it.

That's the next step, he thought. *I have to start putting this all into practice.* The idea was an exciting one, but it was overwhelming too, since he wasn't sure *how.* He had developed no tools for dealing with something like this. Even when he had felt better today, it wasn't because of something he had done; it was the chance meeting of the people in the park that had done it.

He thought about that a little, turning it over in his mind, when his thoughts returned to the voice he had heard. *What was that?*

The voice spoke again suddenly, as if by thinking about it he had called it up. It startled him so badly that he almost fell off his perch.

"Did you already forget what I said?" it laughed. "I'm the part of you Freedom told you about!"

"You almost made me fall out of the tree! Don't you ever pay attention to where I am when you show up?" But Mystic was already regretting his outburst. He had just this moment decided to try to be happier, and already he was yelling at invisible voices. And not only that, he must look like a complete fool, high up in a tree screaming at nothing. If anyone could see him, they'd think he was crazy. Once again, he started to wonder if maybe he *was*.

"Be careful, Mystic, if you lose the sense of ease you've reached, you'll lose me again. Then I won't be able to help you."

"It can't bother you that much, or you wouldn't scare me every time you show up," Mystic said abruptly, surprised he was still carrying on a conversation with the voice. The anxiety was starting to kick in again, and he felt like bolting from the tree as he had from the park, just running away from it all.

"Mystic, you're losing me." By the tone of the voice Mystic could tell it was poking fun at him.

Why is this thing always happy? His irritation began to rise. But instead of following the thought down into negativity, he took deep breaths and began to restore the sense of ease he had lost.

"That's it, Mystic, that's better."

"Please, just go away," Mystic said in between deep breaths.

And all at once it did. He was left alone in the top of the tree, listening to the gentle breeze rattle the leaves.

48

Can I control that voice? Did it actually listen to me just now? But there was no way of knowing the answer and for a while, Mystic didn't dare move or even think. His entire body was tensed and ready to jump again when the voice came back. But it didn't. Feeling certain that it wouldn't come back, he relaxed and breathed normally.

He was beginning to get tired. It was a lot for one morning, but even so, Mystic felt his life was on the verge of changing for the better. He felt that the power Freedom had told him about was near, maybe just around the corner.

He couldn't wait to find Bumpa and share all of this with him.

Tiny

3

A FIRST TASTE OF HAPPINESS

-1-

Mystic had fallen asleep imagining how he and Bumpa would reunite, how Bumpa would laugh and jump when Mystic told him his story. And when he woke, for the first time since Bumpa left, his thoughts were not that Bumpa was gone but rather eagerness to practice a better attitude.

But first, I'm hungry. Mystic had never had to find his own meals before, and he had no idea where to even begin looking. Back at home, his family always made sure his food dish was full when it should be, but he wasn't ready to go home yet. Not until he had changed and had discovered his power.

He knew Sarah would be unhappy not seeing him for a while, but he also knew Jean was a good mother and had already found a way to help Sarah be patient and wait for him. Nonetheless, Mystic felt sad for her. He could clearly see her sitting on the floor of her room playing with her hairdresser set, looking up to the bed where he usually sat, becoming ever sadder not finding him there.

A thought struck him then. He was doing to Sarah what Bumpa had done to him, and he had been so angry at Bumpa for it. The irony was pretty amusing. He laughed. It was as if this had all been plotted out in order to make him realize how selfish and silly he had been.

51

He hoped Sarah would be more understanding than he had been with Bumpa. Sarah was a bighearted little girl—the biggest he had ever met—and she would deal with it better than he had. She would only worry about him, not get angry. Once again, his cheeks flushed pink beneath his fur.

-2-

Mystic sauntered into the clearing where the wild cats were gathered, eating. He knew they'd be pleased to share with him, and with the thought of food his stomach growled loudly.

"Hey, everyone!" Tiger shouted. "It looks like our friend finally smelled the food!" Everyone laughed.

"Yes, I'm starving!" Mystic said cheerfully.

He was surprised by his comfortable response. Before today, he would have been annoyed by Tiger's sarcasm and everyone else's laughter, but he was in such a good mood that it didn't bother him at all. And he had to admit, it felt wonderful to be this way. He didn't feel as though they were laughing at his expense or making fun of him as he used to. All he sensed was their happiness and desire to laugh and joke about anything and everything. They were laughing to lighten the atmosphere, not to belittle him or make him feel bad.

And besides, he thought, *these cats haven't had the advantages I have. They don't have an easy life—if the woman doesn't bring them anything, they have to find food. They have to find protection from predators especially at night...*Thinking about how difficult their lives were in comparison to his made him ashamed. *I can't believe I was playing the victim the way I was. These cats have to work hard to stay alive and happy. Out here it is life and death.*

Mystic looked down at his paws, too embarrassed to meet anyone's eyes. In that moment, he was grateful none of them could read his mind and know how selfish he'd been.

Dusty approached with enthusiasm. "It's great to see you in such good shape!"

"Incredible things have happened to me!" Mystic said.

"Have you seen the black lady cat again? The one who said all those things about feelin' good?" It was a small black cat named Tiny who said this last. He'd been tossed over the park fence a few weeks ago with his brothers and sisters, and in the weeks since, children had seen them and scooped them up one by one. All except for Tiny. The group of wild cats had seen him there alone and adopted him into their group, but Mystic had only met him a few times before now. He had never spoken to him before.

"Yes, Tiny, I have seen her again," Mystic replied. "Her name is Freedom. She tried to help me, but I was too scared and selfish, and I didn't appreciate her help as I should have."

"What about Bumpa?" Dusty asked. "Have you found him?"

"No, not yet." Mystic smiled.

"Have you accepted his departure then?" asked Tiny with wide and gleaming eyes. "Is that why you seem so much better? After they adopted me, the other cats said that, if I accept what is happening to me instead of resistin' it, I can be happy again."

53

Mystic remembered that, after his brothers and sisters were adopted, Tiny had been feeling rejected and angry. Back then, Mystic had been too self-absorbed to really pay attention to what Tiny was going through, and so had never asked if the wild cats' advice had worked for him or not. But now he was curious, not only because it might help him, but because he wanted to know if Tiny was all right.

Mystic thought about Tiny's question. It was interesting.

"I don't know if I've accepted it, Tiny," he said. "I haven't really thought about it yet, so I can't answer. What about you? Have you accepted your siblings' departure?"

Tiny puffed out his chest slightly. "Yes, I have!"

"Really? That's incredible. And how did you do that?"

"I just told myself there was nothin' I could do about it." Tiny spoke quickly and confidently, and Mystic could tell he was excited to be sharing his experience, especially with an older cat. He found himself touched by Tiny's enthusiasm.

Tiny went on happily, "I didn't want to think about all the bad stuff that happens. I like feeling good, and I wanted my brothers and sisters to feel good. Gettin' angry at them for having safe homes to live in was just hurting *me*, so I stopped and stuff got better."

For a second, Mystic was speechless. Hearing so much wisdom and good sense from such a pint-sized little kitten was amazing and beautiful.

"And just look," Tiny said, "I got adopted by the best group of cats in the whole park!"

Dusty, Tiger, and a few of the others surrounded him and chimed in, shouting things like "Absolutely!" and "Without a doubt!" Tiny giggled.

"I'm impressed that you're still sane," Mystic said when he finally found his voice again. "I would have gone nuts going through what you did."

Tiny waved at the group of smiling wild cats. "It's all because of my wonderful family."

"We taught you, Tiny, that's true," Tiger said when the racket died down. "But it's *you* who did all the work. You did it! Not us or anybody else."

Mystic looked at the group of cats as though for the first time and discovered something a little troubling. "How come you all have this knowledge about emotions and our ability to control them and I don't? Or didn't before, anyway." He was starting to feel silly again. When Freedom had first come to him in front of these cats, he had mistaken their silence for confusion. But it turned out that they *had* understood. He was the only one who had been confused.

"I don't know," Dusty said. "Normally, every cat knows these things. Either that or they just need a reminder, like Tiny here." She patted Tiny's head.

Mystic felt his face pulling from a smile to a frown.

Dusty clearly noticed because she quickly added, "But we strongly believe there's a happy reason for this. And we can't wait to discover what will happen with you. We feel it's going to be big and really exciting!"

And just like that, the happiness Mystic had woken up with was back and he was smiling like a loon. "Wow!" he whispered as hope flooded his body.

The wild cats laughed in a loud chorus, came to him one by one, and patted him gently on the head as if welcoming him to his new way of thinking. Mystic was almost dizzy receiving so much great attention all at once. He, who thought he needed to be in pain for others to pay attention to him. He, who thought he would lose everyone's attention if he was happy. He had never been so glad to be proved wrong. He was fulfilled, he had never received such positive attention, and that wasn't a coincidence.

-3-

By the time the last cat patted his head, Mystic was starving. There was still plenty of food scattered on the plates and under the bushes. The woman who brought it was always very generous. There was enough for everyone to eat their fill. And after their bellies were as full as they could stand, the after-dinner ritual of lying down and enjoying the sensation of being satiated commenced.

Mystic selected another large maple close by, climbed it, and settled in the fork where the largest branch connected with the trunk. He curled himself up in such a way that he could see Tiny sleeping in the neighboring tree just in front of him.

He was still very excited about his new way of seeing things, as if everything was so much clearer than before. He could see all the good in others that he hadn't before. He had been too focused on what he didn't like about them or the things they didn't do for him (that he thought they should). He also very much enjoyed being able to listen to their stories with genuine curiosity and interest. And Tiny's story was incredible! Mystic was shocked that he had never heard it all, never really *wanted* to, because he was too focused on his little pains and annoyances.

He had been around the wild cats many times, but today was the first time he had showed them interest and it felt wonderful.

Mystic was amazed that, by focusing only on the bad things and those that didn't work out the way he wanted them to, he had only been able to see those things. He had missed out on all the best things happening around him as well.

A wild smile sprung onto his face. He was filled with hope that the future would be so much more amazing than he could anticipate.

-4-

The following morning, Mystic saw Tiny watching some children playing under the tree he had slept in. Children could sometimes be frightening because most of them had only played with their stuffed animals and didn't understand that real cats—especially small ones—were much more fragile. But Mystic knew the reward of sharing his life with a child.

Tiny would love Sarah, he thought. *They're both so much alike, so full of life and spontaneity yet gentle at the same time.*

Thinking about Sarah made him miss her, and he thought how lucky he was that he had grown up with such a loving family. When Sarah had been a baby, she had been very sweet, but Jean had taught her how to play gently with Mystic. And Jean had taught him how to play with soft paws because of Sarah's delicate skin. She had been kind and patient, and they had learned quickly.

I really have been lucky.

As Mystic watched Tiny watching the children, an idea came to him. He thought about it for a moment, and then a little bit more, and the more he thought the more excited he became. Never before had he had an idea that sparked with such intensity and energy. Soon he couldn't think about it anymore. He had to act.

He scampered down the trunk and ran toward Dusty, who was stretching her back legs beneath the great elm tree she had spent the night in.

"Dusty! Hey, Dusty!" Mystic shouted as he ran.

"Whoa! What's going on?" Dusty said with pleasant curiosity, her eyes still half closed.

"I've just had the best idea in my whole life!"

"I see."

"Oh, I'm so excited!" Mystic bounced up and down on the grass. The energy from this idea was bubbling inside him, and he felt that, if he had to sit still, he would burst. He wanted to share it, to shout it out loudly, but he knew he shouldn't. Not yet anyway. "Is there somewhere more private we can talk about it?"

"Oh, it's a secret, is it?" Dusty said with a sly smile.

"Well, just for now. I want to tell you and then have you talk to the others about it. If you're willing, that is."

"Okay, sure. Let's head toward the park. I know a quiet area down there."

Mystic followed Dusty to a small patch of grass a little out of the way. The children didn't use it, because it was much too small to play on, and at this time of the morning no other cats or birds were around. Along one side was a low wall separating the park from the street, and they sat there in its shadow where it was cool and quiet.

"Okay, we're alone, so what is it?" Dusty asked.

"It won't take long to tell you." Mystic laughed, relishing the moment. His idea was going to change his life—and Tiny's, too.

"Well, don't keep me in suspense any longer," Dusty laughed, too. "What is it?"

"I'm going to take Tiny home with me so he can be adopted by Jean and Pete! Tiny will take my place at the house and become Sarah's friend!" Mystic smiled wider than he ever had before, feeling goofy and wonderful. He stayed that way, waiting for Dusty to react.

Finally, with a baffled look, Dusty did. "But what about you, Mystic? Why would you give away your place in the house, and the comfort you have there, to Tiny?

"Because I'll be too busy looking for Bumpa," Mystic said, serious now. "I need to find him. I need to see that he's okay and know what his days are like now. After that I can go back home and let all that uncertainty go."

"How do you know that Jean and Pete will adopt Tiny?"

"If I bring him to them, they won't be able to refuse."

Dusty was quiet for a moment and then cleared her throat. Mystic couldn't believe it, but she was getting choked up.

"I'm really touched, Mystic," she said. "I want Tiny to be happy, and I think this would make him happy. Even though he's trying really hard to be like us, deep down he's not a wild cat. He's much more like you and Ulysses. He'd thrive in a house like yours with a kid like Sarah."

Mystic leapt to his feet and spun in an excited circle. "See, I told you it was my best idea ever!"

"Don't you want to take at least a day to think about this before we tell everyone? What happens if you change your mind?"

"I don't want to think that way, worrying about what-ifs," Mystic said. "I know this is what I want to do. I don't have a single doubt that it's right. All I want is to enjoy knowing that Sarah and Tiny will be together. They both need this, and they need it now."

Dusty studied Mystic's face for a moment and then broke into a smile. "Okay then. If you're sure, let's go tell the others."

She stood and placed her paw on Mystic's shoulder and Mystic felt her gratitude and appreciation in that gesture. "You're welcome," he said with a wink, and they returned to share his idea.

-*5*-

Being a leader, Dusty presented Mystic's idea. She also spoke about his generosity and courage at length. Mystic blushed a little and again thought of how wonderful it felt to have attention for something positive he had done.

The others greeted this news with loud shouts and whoops of happiness. Their positivity radiated out like waves, and it made him more pleased about his decision to take Tiny home.

Tiny sat speechless, but as soon as Dusty was done speaking, he bounded to his feet, hooked both front legs around Mystic's neck, and squeezed.

"Hey, hey Tiny," Mystic gasped out of breath. "I can't breathe." Tiny released his grasp, and they burst out laughing. After the excitement and euphoria died down, Mystic spent the day explaining to Tiny the kind of life he was about to experience with his new family and house.

Also, to help Tiny be accepted by the family faster, Mystic went through all the house rules with him and even taught him how to play with soft paws. They practiced that together, and by the third fake fight, Tiny was doing much better at controlling his claws, which seemed to want to spring out on their own.

The other cats watched with frowns. Mystic guessed this must all seem so strange to them—intentionally not using their claws or being allowed out of the house to roam where they might want. To live with Jean and Pete would probably seem like a punishment to many of them who had never known anything other than the freedom they had and loved.

As the sun dipped toward the horizon, Mystic turned to Tiny, who was practicing playing with soft paws with another wild cat (who didn't really understand the concept), and said it was time they start for home.

"So soon?" Tiny's voice was full of apprehension, but Mystic could see the excitement that burned in his eyes.

"It'll be fine," Mystic said. "Before you know it, you'll be back here sharing new stories with your friends and wondering why you were worried at all."

That was enough to get Tiny moving. He went around to all the others assembled before him and said his emotional goodbyes.

Before long, Mystic and Tiny were walking side by side out of the park. Tiny turned and looked at the cats behind them, who were all watching with smiling, tearful faces, and waved warmly to them.

"I'll be back soon!" Tiny shouted. "I'll have so much to tell you!"

Mystic smiled and thought, *If you only knew how many stories you'll have.*

-6-

The walk to Mystic's house was a short one. At the edge of the park, they jumped the wall and crossed the road just beyond. It was a quiet street lined with small, well-kept houses, and the people who lived there always drove slowly. Even still, Mystic took the time to explain how to safely cross a road to Tiny, who had never seen one outside the park before.

Once on the other side, they entered a nicely landscaped yard with a low wooden fence at the back. Mystic led Tiny to the fence and jumped. They landed at the back of another yard and stared up at a brightly lit house painted a light cream color.

"It looks like a cream cake!" Tiny said happily.

"This is my home and soon yours, too," Mystic said. "Let's go in."

But Tiny wasn't moving. He seemed frozen to the spot.

His excitement had given way to a look of fear.

Mystic nudged him gently with his head. "Hey, it's okay, don't worry. They really are nice people. They're gentle and kind, so don't be afraid to—"

But before he could finish his thought, the back door opened and Sarah's face appeared.

"Mystic!" She ran toward them across the yard. Frozen in place, Tiny appeared to Mystic like a carving of a kitten instead of a real one. Not even his fur moved as Sarah approached.

"Mommy! Mommy, Mystic's back!"

Mystic realized that Sarah was so focused on him she hadn't even seen Tiny. He stepped behind Tiny and nudged him forward with his head. He wanted to push him right into Sarah's arms if he could.

But it was like pushing against a stone. Tiny's body was so stiff there was almost no give to it at all. But then all at once, he managed to push him off-balance, and Tiny stumbled a few inches forward.

Sarah stopped mid-sprint and stared at them.

"Oooooh!" Her voice melted from loud and rambunctious to soft like silk. "A kitty!" She moved again but very slowly now, and as she got closer, she leaned down so her face was almost on the same level as Tiny's.

"Go over to her, Tiny," Mystic whispered from behind. "Go on." Tiny took three deep breaths and finally moved forward. "That's it, you're doing great! Go and greet her!"

Sarah had sat down in the grass and crossed her legs, and Mystic understood at once why. *She must sense his fear.* She knew he was afraid and letting him come to her on his terms.

He was once again struck by her sensitivity and intelligence.

Mystic heard a door creak and looked up. Jean was standing in the open doorway, watching the scene on the grass below. It was too dark to see her face, but he hoped everything would go as he had planned. Now was the crucial time.

Tiny had stopped in the grass a few feet from Sarah and was just sitting there, looking at her.

Sarah called, "Mystic! Mystic come see me!" in a loud whisper.

And Mystic was so happy to see her, to be back where he felt at home, that he couldn't resist her any longer. He went to her and let her pick him up. It was so wonderful to be there, to be squeezed and cherished. He looked down at Tiny and winked.

It's the perfect way to reassure him and show him there's nothing to be afraid of, he thought and was surprised to see Tiny moving forward again.

Tiny crawled cautiously to Sarah and rubbed his head against her knees. Sarah beamed, but she didn't move. Then Tiny tried very awkwardly to leap up into her lap. Mystic saw that he jumped without using his claws, though, and he slipped right off, fell backward into the grass, and landed upside down, legs splayed in the air.

Sarah burst out laughing. Tiny jerked around and backed up a few steps at the sound.

"I'm sorry, kitty," Sarah said tenderly. "I didn't mean to scare you, but you are too funny." She laughed again but more softly this time.

Before Mystic could check on Tiny to see if he was okay

(and reassure him if he wasn't), he heard footsteps. He craned his neck to look over Sarah's shoulder.

Jean was approaching.

Mystic squeezed his eyes shut tight and thought over and over, *Let's hope it works, let's hope it works!*

-7-

Jean's voice startled him and he opened his eyes. "Okay, okay, what's going on down here?" she said.

Tiny let out a little squeak of fear and hid behind Sarah's left knee. Sarah smiled and let out a giggle. She seemed delighted that, in a moment of danger, Tiny had trusted her to protect him. It was a good sign for their relationship.

"Mommy, look!" She held Mystic out to Jean. "He came back!"

"And not alone, it would seem." Jean nodded at Tiny, who was still crouched behind Sarah's knee.

"Isn't he cute, Mommy?" Mystic was so in tune with Sarah he could tell just by the sound of her voice that she was gearing up to beg Jean for the kitten to stay.

"Sure, Sarah, he's very cute—all the kittens in the whole world are very cute—but it doesn't mean we can adopt them all."

"Oh please!" Sarah said, setting Mystic down on the grass and jumping to her feet. She clasped her hands together as if she were about to pray. "Please can't he stay with us? My friend Mary has two cats, and she said it's not much more work than one! Please?"

65

"Grandma won't agree to look after two cats when we leave for vacation, Sarah. For *her* it will be overwhelming"

"We can ask someone else then?"

"Sarah..."

As Sarah and Jean's discussion ping-ponged on, Mystic assessed their body language, especially Jean's tone of voice. He felt she wasn't really thrilled with the idea of adopting another cat.

Sarah's begging intensified. She bounced with concern and whined even more.

Tiny looked at Mystic with fear and worry in his eyes.

Suddenly, Mystic got another idea. He was certain it would work. But they had to act right away.

"I'm going to leave," he whispered to Tiny, whose face flooded with immediate panic.

"No! Don't leave me alone, not yet!"

Mystic looked at Sarah, who was still trying to change her mother's mind. Tiny and Sarah whined just the same way, and it made him laugh.

"What's so funny?" Tiny asked.

"You have no idea yet that this place is your home and how much you and Sarah will thrive living with each other."

Tiny sighed. Mystic let him gather his courage.

"Okay, Mystic," Tiny let out with resolution in his voice. "I trust you. You've told me so many amazing things about this family, and I believe it will be as good as you say it will. I'm still nervous about doin' this without you, but I'm ready to try."

"I'd love to stay here and help you, too," Mystic said, his throat tight, "but the only way for you to be adopted is for me to leave now." Sarah and Jean had just stopped talking, and seeing Sarah's sad frown, Mystic knew it was time. He looked back at Tiny, who nodded that he was ready.

Mystic walked a little way away and meowed loudly. He had found that this was the best way of getting the family's attention whenever he needed food or love.

At once, Jean and Sarah faced him.

"You see, Mommy?" Sarah whined. "Mystic is crying because he wants us to keep the baby."

"Sweetie, cats don't understand what we say," Jean said. "Just as we can't fully understand them. Mystic has no idea that we're discussing not keeping the kitten—"

"Or keeping it!" Sarah cut her off. But both were stunned to silence when Mystic went behind Tiny and nudged him forward with his head. "You see, Mommy! Mystic *does* understand!"

Jean didn't respond. As Mystic pushed Tiny across the small patch of grass between them, Jean watched, completely fascinated. It was what he had hoped would happen.

Mystic nudged Tiny another couple of feet until he was right in front of Jean and then stopped. "All right, Tiny," he whispered, "I've done everything I can. You have to take it from here. And don't worry, either—I can tell it's working. I can read it on Jean's face."

Without waiting for Tiny to respond, Mystic turned around, walked three determined steps toward the wooden fence, and stopped. He looked back at Jean and Sarah.

"Mom? What's he doing?"

Jean shook her head, bewildered. "I don't know,

sweetheart. But for sure he's telling us he wants us to keep this kitten."

Mystic faced the wooden fence again, advanced three steps, and stopped once more to look back at them.

"Mystic!" Sarah called, her voice shaking. Even from as far away as he was, Mystic could hear the sadness beginning to engulf her. "Are you leaving again?"

Mystic could sense that she needed to be comforted. He meowed at her, and she ran down the yard and tried to grab him up, but he deftly avoided her hands. Her face froze and crumpled at the perceived snub, but he jumped on her feet and rubbed himself against her legs. He didn't want to hurt her.

Sarah knelt beside him in the grass, tears falling from her eyes as she started to stroke him. "Why Mystic?" she sobbed. "Why do you want to leave me?"

Mystic felt all her pain. He meowed again and rubbed himself against her legs. It was all he could do to comfort her.

Jean had walked up behind Sarah while she and Mystic were saying their goodbyes, and Tiny plodded alongside her. "I don't think he wants to leave you, Sarah," she said. "It looks to me like he has something he needs to do. He came to say that he loves you, and he even brought you a friend to keep you company while he's gone."

Jean looked at Tiny, knelt down, and petted him on the head. Tiny tensed at first, but after a moment he began to purr. Mystic knew from experience how soft and kind Jean's hands were and that this was a totally new and unique experience for Tiny. The kitten glanced at Mystic with wide, unbelieving eyes. Mystic could almost hear him asking in his squeaky little voice, *is this really happening?*

Mystic nodded to confirm that it actually was. *Here you go, my friend.*

Sarah was still sobbing while kissing and caressing Mystic. "Will he come back?"

"I'm sure that, when he finishes whatever he has to do, he will," Jean said. "He has every other time, hasn't he?" There was something in her voice that Mystic couldn't quite place, but he thought Jean might be trying to convince herself of what she was saying as much as Sarah.

Sarah leaned down and placed her lips against Mystic's ear. "Come back, come back, come back," she whispered to him.

He meowed again.

"I love you too, Mystic." Sarah scooped him into her arms and squeezed him hard. He let her do it this time and enjoyed it.

"It looks like you've gained another furry friend, courtesy of Mystic," Jean said. Tiny was in her arms, sitting patiently and still purring, and she offered him over to Sarah. Sarah planted one last kiss on Mystic's forehead, set him down on the grass, and gathered Tiny into her arms.

"I'm impressed, Mystic," Jean said. "You're a very smart little cat. It's almost as though you planned this whole thing." She smiled down at him knowingly.

Mystic could feel her kindness, and he meowed at her, which made her smile even wider.

"I'm going to cherish him," Sarah said between her tears, holding Tiny up to Mystic. Mystic knew everything was fine then.

"Don't forget to come back to me," Sarah said, now in Jean's arms with Tiny held between them.

"Yes, come back anytime," Jean said.

He turned and jumped to the top of the wooden fence, looked back one last time at his family and his home, and then leapt down on the other side.

-*8*-

Mystic landed on the grass at the bottom of the fence and stopped to take stock before heading back to the park. He couldn't believe he had actually done it. He'd had the idea only this morning to install Tiny in his home while he was gone, and it had come to fruition quickly and easily. It felt unreal. He'd given his home away. It was terrifying, but at the same time, he told himself, it was only temporary. He *had* to find Bumpa and see him in his new life. Not only that, he was giving a kitten the life he had always dreamed about having, and that thought filled Mystic with joy.

And after what he had discovered and implemented in the last three days, something was pushing him to take this adventure even further.

It was worth leaving his comfortable life behind for a while.

Thinking about his journey and the exciting hope of finding Bumpa, Mystic no longer felt scared. He was actually starting to feel confident.

Wanting to keep up his positive mood, he decided to return to the other cats to tell them about Tiny's new home.

When he entered the park, he saw they were still sitting there, waiting for him in almost the same places they had been when he and Tiny had left. They hadn't seen him yet and most wore a look of apprehension. The moment he entered the clearing alone, that look disappeared entirely and a raucous cheer went up into the night sky.

Dusty, sitting near the front of the crowd, ran over to Mystic. "So? How did it go? Tell us what happened! Tell us everything!" The others near the front cried out in agreement.

Mystic was amused that they had all sat there just waiting for news of what had happened to Tiny, and he was once again touched by their kindness.

He moved to the center of a rough circle of cats, sat on the grass, and told them the tale from start to finish. The other cats seemed to hang on his every word, and some even laughed when he told them about nudging Tiny forward to convince Jean to keep him.

When he was done, there was a moment of silence broken only when Tiger stepped forward and asked, "So how are you feeling now you've left Tiny and your family behind?"

Mystic thought about it for a moment. "Well, at first I was deeply sad. Leaving Sarah behind was such a hard thing, and after that I was scared. It felt almost like something was missing inside me and it had left a hole that made it hard to breathe. It was a crushing feeling, and I was afraid I wouldn't overcome it."

"And now?" Tiger asked. "Can you still feel that emptiness and pain?"

Everyone around them stiffened visibly, and the atmosphere became tense. Mystic thought they were reacting as though he were made of fine china and would break at the slightest touch. It amused him.

"Well, if you make me think about it, it will come back for sure!" Mystic snorted. And just like that, the tension was broken. The other cats even began to laugh, and Dusty, who was standing behind Tiger, winked at Mystic in approval.

"So you've really made the link between what you think and what you feel?" Tiger asked, surprised.

"Yes!" Mystic said with pride. "What I think influences how I feel."

"So, then you realize that, if you always think about pleasant things, you'll always feel good?" Tiger asked.

"No," Mystic said after a thought. "At first, the situation caused an outburst of emotions—it was leaving Tiny behind with my family that induced the pain and panic. It wasn't anything I thought." He paused. The atmosphere had tensed again, as if they were waiting for a happy ending to the story. It satisfied him and made him feel powerful to be commanding all of their attention. "It was only once the situation was behind me that my emotions could be influenced by what I was thinking."

The others relaxed again, and he decided to finish the story on a high note. "If I had dwelled on the pain and fear I felt about leaving my life behind, I would have been stuck there as if I had walked in glue. But I started to think about finding Bumpa again, and that caused the fear to disappear, replaced by excitement instead."

"I think you've got it, kid!" Tiger said excitedly. "So, tell us, how are you going to find Bumpa?"

Mystic felt as though he'd just been slapped. He hadn't thought yet about how to find Bumpa—hadn't even considered it—and Tiger's question had thrown him. "Well...well, I..." he stammered as the other cats watched him. He felt his good mood melting away. "I don't know yet...I just don't know."

"Hey, don't worry," Tiger said quickly. "You'll figure it out, kid. It will come to you in no time."

"But how?" Mystic, felt his anger for the first time since yesterday. He was beginning to hate Tiger and all his nosy questions. They were screwing up his sense of wellbeing.

Tiger smiled. "If you keep practicing positive thinking, everything will come to you fast and easily."

Mystic didn't want to hear it; he was really becoming frustrated and angry. "As if feeling good could tell me where to go and what to do to find Bumpa!"

"Never underestimate the power of your happiness, Mystic."

Mystic was taken aback by Tiger's seriousness and didn't dare say anything else. A part of him wanted to understand more of what Tiger was talking about, but a larger part was hungry and tired and didn't feel like talking at all.

Dusty cleared her throat in an exaggerated way and tried to change the subject. "How about some dinner and a good night's sleep?" she said.

As everyone stood and headed toward the feeding area, Mystic was happy to no longer be the center of attention.

Even though he was hungry, he didn't think he could eat

anything right now, so while the others all went off in one direction, he headed in the other, intent on taking a walk around the park to clear his head. As he wandered, dragging his feet, he recalled everything that had happened since leaving his home tonight.

When he had thought about being back with Bumpa, he had forgotten about being realistic about the situation. He had only imagined the end result where they were back together and happy again.

But that was just an illusion. In reality there was no way he could find Bumpa. *How can I?* he thought. *How can a cat find an elephant taken away, who knows where, three days ago? And not just moved from one place to another in the park, but loaded into a truck and taken far away?*

He felt more and more pain every second, and with each step he took, Bumpa felt farther and farther away. He knew he should try to think about something else to change his emotional state, but he was too tired to even try.

I've left my home and my family. And now I'll never see Bumpa again, either. What have I done?

Trembly

4

LOSING FAITH AND FACING FEAR

Mystic was walking in a section of the park he had never been in before. He was feeling incredibly low, all the thoughts of his home and Tiny swirling around like a tornado in his mind, when a red cat jumped out from behind an old gnarled hollow tree.

The cat was imposing, with a wide face scarred from some long ago battle, and he was missing a chunk of his left ear. One eye was deep gray and the other a vibrant emerald green, which gave him an unbalanced look. Mystic didn't recall ever seeing the cat around before, and he certainly would have remembered this one.

"Those cats all say the same thing," the red cat hissed.

"Excuse me?" Mystic had no idea what the cat was talking about, and he was in no mood for guessing games.

"They say that all you have to do is feel good and your life will be like a dream." The red cat burst out laughing, and it was a rather unpleasant sound, like someone sloshing through mud.

"Look, I don't know who you are or what you want, but I'm not in the mood to talk to anyone right now."

The red cat showed all his teeth. "My name is Trembly."

"Glad to hear it, have a good day now." Mystic started to walk away, but Trembly followed him as though he hadn't heard a word.

"Aren't you afraid that you won't have a home ever again now that you've so selflessly given yours away?" he said snidely and chuckled again.

"No, I'm not. Not at all," Mystic said with no real interest. He was sick of thinking and talking about it just now. But as he turned to walk down another path, what Trembly had said struck him. He stopped dead in his tracks and turned.

"Wait, what did you just say?" Mystic's voice pitched dangerously low and his eyes were burning. Trembly should have had no way of knowing about Mystic giving Tiny a place in his home, yet somehow he did.

"I'm just saying it's a pretty simplistic way to view life," Trembly said with a twisted smile.

"Who are you really? And what sort of games are you playing?"

"Like I said, my name is Trembly. And I'm not playing any games. Quite the opposite, actually. I'm here to protect you. The others who keep talking about feeling good are just dragging you further and further from reality, and it's dangerous. You could get lost."

Mystic surveyed the cat in front of him but didn't say a word. There was something odd about him. It wasn't his different colored eyes or the scars that covered him. Many of the wild cats had battle scars and multicolored eyes—it wasn't really all that odd. There was something about *this* cat that just seemed...off. Mystic wasn't sure if he could trust him, but at the same time he felt as though he had known him his whole life.

"And isn't that how you were feeling just now?" Trembly said. "Lost?"

"Well...I mean, yes, but..." Mystic didn't quite know how to finish his thought. He hadn't really felt lost, had he? He wasn't sure anymore.

"You must be careful not to lose sight of the dangers that surround you," Trembly said quietly.

The cat sounded sincere enough to Mystic, but all the same it was strange. Why should he care about Mystic or what happened to him? They'd only just met. It was unsettling.

"Feeling good isn't going to protect you from danger." Trembly took a step closer until their faces were almost touching, and Mystic could see the glint in his green eye. "It even caused you to act in a way that put you in more danger than you were in before. I mean, look at you now. You have no family, no home—"

"I can go back whenever I want to!" Mystic said. "It's still my home! I've always been welcome there, and I know I can go back anytime!"

"You're not afraid that they'll change their minds?" Trembly looked at Mystic out of the corner of his eye. It made him appear shifty, and Mystic didn't care for that at all. "After all, Tiny's a *verrrrry* cute little guy, isn't he? It would be easy for them to decide to keep a cute little kitten like that and leave you outside. I've seen it before, you know. You're four—that's practically ancient..."

"They would never do that!" Mystic shouted suddenly with great force. "Sarah would never let that happen!" Trembly was saying what Mystic didn't quite dare even

79

think, and each word was like a barb in his side.

"Sarah, Sarah, Sarah," Trembly said, shaking his head from side to side. "She is only a child, after all, and very impressionable. It's possible she might think that Tiny, being so small, might need extra care and attention, and then she'd have no time for you. Besides, she isn't the one making the decisions, is she? It's her parents you have to worry about."

"Go away!" Mystic's voice echoed in the quiet night air. "Just go away and leave me alone!"

"Of course." Trembly kept smiling his toothy smile. "Just know that, when you need me, I'll be around. And trust me, you will need me before too long." With that, he leapt very agilely behind the tree from which he had appeared and was gone, leaving Mystic alone with his thoughts, more shaken up than ever.

-2-

Mystic crouched in the grass and shook like a leaf.

What did I do? Oh what did I do? All I wanted was to find Bumpa, to be happy again! But they all tried to convince me I didn't have to find Bumpa to be happy.

Mystic sighed, exasperated. *And then those wild cats took advantage of me and manipulated me because they needed to find Tiny a home! Trembly is right! And now they've messed everything up!*

The park around him suddenly seemed darker and stranger than it had before. The thought of having to live here from now on instead of in his comfortable home with his family was almost too much to bear.

He was thinking about this when a loud, sudden snap, like the breaking of a dead branch, came from the bushes to his left. Mystic didn't stick around to find out what it was. As soon as the sound came, he was off and running, so worked up and full of fear and anger that he didn't even have time to think before he was in motion. It was only once he was on his way that he discovered he was heading back to where the wild cats had been gathered.

It was a short run, especially moving as quickly as he was, and in no time he saw them. They were still milling around and talking to one another where he had left them. As soon as the first cat was in sight, Mystic could contain his anger no longer. His rage at them exploded when they were still just gray blurs in the darkness.

"How could you do that to me?" he shouted.

All the cats within earshot stopped what they were doing and turned to Mystic, their ears flattened against their skulls.

"What will I do now?" he roared. "What will I do now?" He was running out of breath but still managed to keep going. "Did you do this because you wanted me to stay here and live with you?" He stopped quickly in front of Dusty, kicking up a spume of dirt. "I had a life and you destroyed it!" he snapped in her face. "You used me for your own good and to get a home for Tiny! How could you? How could you do that to me?"

His rage was ebbing quickly, and so was his strength. When he ran into the clearing, he had felt full of energy and anger, but now with all his anger screamed out, he was hollow and unable to support his own weight. He collapsed onto the grass and placed his paws over his head. "I'll never be happy again," he said in a small voice very different from the roar he had just used. He began to sob uncontrollably.

"Hey, hey, hey, what's going on, love?" Dusty said.

Mystic looked up at her with teary eyes. His head felt like it weighed a thousand pounds. "How can you call me *love* after everything you did to me?"

"What are you talking about? Take your time and tell me everything that's happened since you left, okay?"

Mystic nodded as best as he could. "I met this cat," he said, still sobbing and gasping, but it was beginning to subside now. "He explained how all of this 'feeling good' stuff was a way for you to manipulate me. That you were trying to make me feel invulnerable, and then I would give my home away to Tiny."

"I see," Dusty said, nodding. "And it would seem by your reaction that you believed this cat, didn't you?"

"Of course I did!" Mystic's voice was hoarse and he no longer had the strength to be as loud as he wanted to be. "Everything the other cat told me was true. You did make me feel invulnerable, and I did give my home away as a result. I gave the only happy thing I had now that Bumpa's gone. And you made me believe I could find Bumpa and that I wouldn't need my home for a while, and you also made me believe I could go back when this is all over..." Mystic had to stop again and catch his breath because he was getting so worked up. Dusty waited patiently.

"This cat, Trembly, he told me that my family would choose Tiny over me if I tried to go back to them," Mystic said when he was able. Saying it out loud made it seem even more real, and he felt warm teardrops staining his fur.

Dusty stepped forward with a look of compassion, but he stopped her before she could get too close.

"Stay where you are! I don't trust you anymore."

"All of this is in your head," she said kindly. "This cat, Trembly, only exists because of your doubt. You're letting your fears take over and get the better of you."

"I don't believe you anymore," Mystic said. "Nothing you say makes sense. But what Trembly told me is real—it's the truth. I can see it and touch it. Tiny is at home with my family, while I'm here with no one and nowhere to go. *This* is the reality. *This* is the truth."

"The confidence and wellbeing you felt were also real, Mystic. And it's because it was real and you felt it so intensely that you were invulnerable and decided to act the way you did."

"Because you manipulated me."

"There was no manipulation. Tiny would have found a home when it was right for him to; we didn't need to force it to happen. And besides, I even asked if you really wanted to wait to take Tiny home, do you remember? You told me you didn't want to wait. It was your decision, Mystic."

"You should have tried harder," Mystic said sullenly. He knew Dusty was right—she *had* asked him if he was sure, and Mystic had said he was—but he was still too angry and scared to admit it. He wanted Dusty to be responsible for the whole thing.

She was smiling, infuriatingly calm. "I could have insisted until I was blue in the face, and you wouldn't have changed your mind. You had reached such a powerful state of mind you could have moved mountains if you wanted to, and nothing I or anyone else could have said would have stopped you."

"That power was an illusion!" Mystic shouted. "You manipulated me and lied to me!"

"No, Mystic, you *were* powerful, and if you decide to go back to that state of positivity, you would feel it again. You would *be* powerful again, too."

"Sure," Mystic said. "And this time, maybe I wouldn't just give away my home but maybe my skin, eyes, and organs, too."

"And that would be your choice too," Dusty said. "The only thing that can break you down is your fear, and you're being manipulated by it right now. You're losing your power to your fears. You shouldn't let your actions be determined by what gives you pain but by what gives you relief, hope, and enthusiasm."

Mystic shook his head. "You're nuts."

"She's not," Tiger said from behind him, making him jump. Tiger didn't seem to notice. "Dusty is telling the truth. If you practice feeling good, you will start to feel alive, *really* alive. It's powerful. But if you give into your fears and let them control you, you'll enter an abyss of infinite pain and misery. Once you go too far, no one will be able to help you get back."

"I don't want to hear anymore," Mystic said and found the strength to stand again. "*You* are the ones scaring me, talking about things that are totally incomprehensible...I just don't want to hear anymore." He turned and walked away at a fast pace, not knowing where he was heading but knowing it had to be better than staying here.

"Mystic, the path you're choosing is a difficult one," Dusty called from behind him. Mystic kept walking. "If you continue down it, just know you're going to need a lot of courage."

I'm doing the right thing, Mystic thought. *I have to get as far away from them as possible.* He tried to resign himself to being alone with no home, no family, no friends...It wouldn't be easy, but he had no choice. He couldn't stay here with these cats—there was something wrong with them—and Mystic knew that, if he stayed, he would soon be poisoned in the mind like they were. After all, he had listened to them once, and now everything was a gigantic mess.

"You do what you have to do, Mystic!" Tiger shouted amiably from behind him. "And when you've experienced enough pain and terror, just know you are welcome back here with us—whenever you want!"

Part of him desperately wanted to turn and stay with them—they knew how to feed and protect themselves, which he didn't—but all the same, he knew he had to keep going.

"One last thing!" Tiger shouted from far away now. "Don't put too much stock in what Trembly tells you!"

Mystic paused. The thought of the large red cat was frightening. *Why is he saying that I'll see Trembly again?* he wondered. The idea of encountering Trembly out there in the dark somewhere made him reconsider leaving for a moment.

No, he thought finally. *No, it's better to leave and deal with it head-on if it comes to that. Those cats are nuts, and I need to figure out what's going on—without their influence.*

Mystic walked forward again against all his instincts, which were pulling him backwards, his throat and stomach tight with anxiety.

A while later, Mystic found himself near the edges of his known territory, deep in the trees that grew in the park. The darkness was nearly total. Before, there had been streetlamps in the distance and lights near some of the park enclosures, but now he was in the wilderness, there was nothing but the stars overhead.

As he walked and his anger lowered to a simmer, he felt a gnawing hunger he hadn't noticed before.

He usually loved this time of night. If everything was as it had been, he would just be waking up on Sarah's bed to go off and meet Bumpa. But now he was in an unknown part of the woods, alone, hungry, and almost certainly in danger. He reflected on how his life had turned completely upside down in no time at all.

He walked past a large green trash can by the path, leapt up to the rim, and peered inside. Some of the wild cats found food in these green bins from time to time, and he thought it might be a good place to start looking. After a moment of digging through a cloud of odor, he came up with a partially eaten ham sandwich that smelled good. He gobbled the meat down, leaving the soggy bread on the grass, and hunted out a large tree that would be safe to spend the night in.

Once he was nestled in the crook of the tree, images of Sarah and Bumpa floated up in his mind again. He pushed them away brusquely. What he needed most now was sleep, and the pain of thinking about his friends and family would keep it from him. But the images came back anyway. A few times, he succeeded in getting rid of them, but the space they left behind was filled with other worries—such as what could happen to a cat like him who was alone in the woods. Between the two competing trains of thought, Mystic didn't know if he would ever find a way to fall asleep.

As he was grappling with this, and the prospect of a long and sleepless night, he heard the hard scrabbling of claws on tree bark from below. Mystic stood and arched his back, ready to fight whatever was coming.

"Enjoying your new home?" Trembly sneered. He lay on the branch below, his long red tail flicking lazily as he spoke.

Mystic's heart beat full speed. For a moment, he contemplated running down the tree and back to the wild cats. *They may be crazy, but at least they're safe.* But that would mean getting even closer to the red cat, and Mystic didn't think he could do that. Not yet anyway.

"You can run away from me, but the danger will still follow you," Trembly said as though reading it on Mystic's face. "You don't need to be afraid of me. I'm not dangerous."

Mystic opened his mouth to object, but Trembly cut him off.

"Oh, there's plenty around here that *is* dangerous," he said with another flick of his tail. "The fisher cats, for instance. And then there are great owls that could grab a cat and be gone before you could blink an eye." Mystic shuddered, and Trembly seemed to pick up on it because he went on with great relish, "And don't forget the wild dogs. And then there're some things I can't even name, but you wouldn't want to run into them in the dark, that's for sure. So many dangers for a little cat like you."

Mystic didn't know all the things Trembly was talking about, but his mind compensated by creating horrible monstrous images and showing them to him.

He took a deep breath and peered down into Trembly's eyes. Even that small gesture took almost all the courage he had, and he was glad he was sitting on such a sturdy branch. His legs were quivering beneath him, and a less stable branch would have been wobbling dangerously.

"Dusty said you were an illusion," he said quietly.

Trembly just looked at him with a slight smile and said nothing.

Mystic was feeling a little stronger now. "She also said that, if I found a way to feel better, then you would disappear."

Trembly's icy smile was frozen on his mouth. "Good luck with your first night alone, Mystic," he said finally, laughing and giving his tail one final flick. He stood, stretched, and whispered, "You're going to need it," before bounding down the tree and disappearing.

Mystic stayed tense, watching the ground to see the smudge of red that was Trembly, but he was gone. Finally, his heart began to slow.

But before it reached its normal pace, something overhead erupted with a high-pitched screech, and images of the monsters Trembly had been talking about flickered across his mind. As Mystic twisted his head up to scan the sky, he lost his balance and slid off the branch. Luckily, his reflexes kicked in immediately, and as he tumbled, his paws grabbed for the branch on which he had just been sitting. His nails popped out and into the bark. His right paw latched onto the branch, his left onto the trunk, his muscles aching with the effort of keeping himself attached to the tree.

He had barely registered the fact that he had saved himself from a nasty fall, when the screeching came again, this time much closer.

I have to get out of here!

Without wasting any time, he began to carefully climb down the trunk, but before he had gone more than a few feet, he heard the distinctive rustling of feathers in the breeze. His heart was gripped with icy terror. Whatever kind of bird it was, it was approaching fast and it was aiming for him. Without thinking about what he was doing, he retracted his claws and, after a split second, plummeted down the trunk into the darkness below.

The bird slammed into the tree where he had just been. Mystic heard the talons on bark and felt large chunks of it raining down around him as he fell. The bird let out a frustrated squawk and was gone again with the ominous flutter of wings.

Mystic, sensing the ground rushing up toward him, flipped over so that his feet were pointed down. He landed with a thud and a twinge of pain, but that was secondary to the fear of the flying creature attacking him. He didn't take time to decide but ran blindly through the woods. He didn't care where he ended up; the only thing he wanted was to get as far away from the bird as quickly as he could.

The bird screeched again, and now it sounded to Mystic as though it was coming from directly behind him. He had to find somewhere to hide—and fast. He leapt over a rotten log, running full speed, and as he came down on the other side, spotted a full, leafy bush to his right. It would have to do.

He dove beneath it and had barely concealed himself when he heard the clack of the bird's talons on the branch behind him and the ripping of leaves. Mystic didn't dare move or even breathe, and a few seconds later the screech came again. This time it was from well overhead and farther away.

It must not be able to get in here, he thought, hoping he was right.

The bird continued to screech angrily, and once more Mystic heard the tearing of leaves from somewhere overhead, but still the big bird couldn't get in.

It flew to a branch nearby and squawked in frustration a few more times before Mystic heard the heavy rustling of its wings. Then, its screeches came from farther away until he couldn't hear them at all.

Mystic waited to make sure that the bird was really gone. Minutes passed and, little by little, the sounds of the woods began to return: the chirping of crickets and the scuttling of small creatures running through the underbrush. It was then Mystic knew it was really safe. He crawled out from beneath the bush.

He was relieved for a moment before the same old questions returned to him. It seemed crazy so soon after being attacked like that, but at the same time they were important questions that needed answers. *Now what?* he thought. *Where can I go that's safe? What am I supposed to do?*

"Find something to enjoy," said the voice Mystic hadn't

heard since the last time he had told it to go away. Its appearance now was so close on the tail of the bird attack that Mystic was startled and halfway back to the bush before he realized what it was. Once he did, he was no longer scared. He was irritated.

"Focus on something that makes you feel better," the voice continued in its cheery manner. "Something that—"

"Stop!" Mystic slapped his paws over his ears. "Enough of that stuff, please! Please just stop talking!" He stayed motionless. The voice had stopped.

He exhaled, relieved, and as he was about to remove his paws, the voice spoke again and startled him all over.

"Each time you reach a state of relief, I can help you."

I really am going crazy, Mystic thought. This time he'd heard the voice while his ears were covered by his paws, so there could be no doubt that the voice was coming from inside his own head. *If I'm hearing voices in my head, I really must be going crazy!* He dropped his paws, afraid to hear the voice again, and paced in wide circles in the clearing. *And not only have I heard it, but I talked to it, too! Oh boy, I'm in a big mess here.*

He continued pacing and talking to himself, becoming more and more afraid of what it might mean, until he noticed the forest had once again become quiet. He stopped in his tracks and stared around him.

The wind was rustling last fall's leaves, which were still scattered across the forest floor, but the crickets had ceased their chirping. Then a tree branch cracked. He snapped his head up to look at the dark canopy of trees overhead, but he couldn't make out anything against the darkened sky.

What if the bird is up there right now watching me? That thought was enough to start him running without sticking around to see what had made the noise. The only thing he wanted now was to get out of the woods and back to where there was more life—life that wasn't trying to kill him.

As he ran, he heard the crackling of branches, as if something in the treetops was following his progress. Terror enveloped him as he stumbled along the dark path, tripping over rocks and protruding tree roots. His panicked breath no longer offered enough oxygen. The edges of his vision blurred as he ran on, and whatever was in the trees above continued to chase him.

Finally, he tripped on a large rock sticking up out of the ground and went somersaulting through the weeds before coming to rest on his side. He stared up at the trees, unable to move or even scream.

It looked to him like the very trees were moving on their own.

As he lay on his side, they reached toward him, their branches moving like giants' arms with long, grasping fingers and sharp claws. The longer he watched, the closer they seemed to get until he felt as though he would pass out from the terror. He had never been so frightened in his entire life, and nothing, not even the fear of losing his family or dying of starvation, could compare to the feeling.

His heart was lurching and thumping chaotically. He felt certain this was the end.

There's nothing I can do to stop this.

Mystic closed his eyes. The world was dark beyond his eyelids, and he followed the darkness down as deeply as he could, certain death would be there to greet him at the bottom.

5

INTUITION

-1-

When Mystic opened his eyes the next morning, the sun was still struggling up over the horizon. For a moment he had no idea where he was. The events of the night before were still foggy in his mind.

Maybe I just dreamt it all, he thought, but when he tried to sit up, the sore muscles in his neck, back, and legs told him that he hadn't. Around him the trees didn't look sinister at all. In fact, he couldn't remember a morning where they had looked more beautiful.

I must have fainted. He laughed a little to himself. He'd never fainted before, never even thought it was possible to become so afraid that he would, but that must have been what happened. There was certainly nothing evil in the woods around him now.

A little way off, he saw flashes of blue between the sturdy trunks of the trees, and from the blue he heard the quacking of ducks. He watched as they swam back and forth, content to paddle around in the warm morning light.

Mystic was deeply relaxed, his mind quiet and calm as he had never experienced it. As if the shock he'd had last night had turned it off, and with it all emotions. He couldn't distinguish exactly what he was feeling. He was just here, in this moment, aware of the beauty that surrounded him, wanting for nothing. He discovered that he enjoyed feeling this way—as though nothing mattered anymore. After all, he'd already thought he'd died, and anything else that happened couldn't be worse than that. Thinking this made him smile.

It's really been an interesting couple of days since Bumpa left.

During that time he'd experienced sorrow when he'd lost Bumpa, intense joy when he'd met Freedom and discovered there was a different way to live. He'd given away his home to Tiny, which had caused him anger due to a sense of betrayal. This led to the extreme fear he'd experienced in the woods last night, followed by a total shutdown of his consciousness. And now he was feeling something else new. Complete and total peace.

This state of peacefulness made Mystic feel invulnerable again. *But this time, I won't do anything foolish with it,* he thought.

He was standing there, enjoying his calmness, when he remembered he had also thought he'd gone crazy last night. "That's right," he said aloud. "I kept hearing that voice in my head. But was it really coming from me?"

As soon as the words were out of his mouth, he cringed, expecting the voice to start speaking again. Last night it had told him that, whenever he was feeling better, it would come to help him. And, Mystic noted with growing apprehension, each time he had started to feel better and had asked a question, the voice had popped up and given him an answer. And that was exactly what he had just done.

His paws were already heading toward his ears to cover

them when he heard the voice as clear as day.

"Well," it said with smug satisfaction, "you should know by now that doing *that* won't help."

Mystic sighed. "I guess my good time is over, isn't it?"

"If you choose it to be," the voice giggled.

Mystic could feel his irritation growing again, quickly replacing his feeling of peacefulness.

"No," he replied as calmly as he could, dreading the loss of calmness. "I am not choosing anything here. You're the one responsible for my misery." He paused and took a deep breath. He really wanted to be alone and enjoy how well he had felt before this voice had come along and disturbed him. "Every time I go through some horrible emotions, manage to get past them, and find a way to feel better, here you come to spoil everything, which is what you are doing right now."

"I'm here because you want help," the voice said sharply.

"No, that's not why you come." Mystic was struggling against his anger at the voice and at himself for engaging with it again. "You come here to get on my nerves and to scare me and to spout all sorts of nonsense."

What am I doing? I'm talking to the voice in my head again.

"Yes, I am within you," the voice said, interrupting Mystic's thoughts. "And you're talking to me not because you're going crazy, but because you know I'm the part of you that knows how to help you find Bumpa, enjoy your life, and find a way to get back home. I am the answer to all your questions."

Mystic didn't know what to say or think. (The voice had

97

heard his thoughts!)

"You're not losing your mind, Mystic. But you are losing me." The voice was less audible now, moving farther away. "You're losing me because you're losing your calm and your peacefulness…" It was barely a whisper now. "You're scared, and I can't help you anymore…"

Mystic waited for a few moments, listening to the silence, dreading the voice showing back up and shattering it, but it seemed to be gone. He wished he could talk to someone about it, about everything that was happening. He missed talking with Bumpa.

Heavy sadness ran through him. He found himself tearing up at the thought of being able to share all his craziness with Bumpa. He no longer had anyone he could share with on that level.

Who else is there? Ulysses is so busy with his family that he wouldn't really have time, and the wild cats…well, they're just as nuts as the voice is, and they would just tell me to listen to it! The thought made him giggle.

"See?" the voice said, startling Mystic once more. "Doesn't it feel better to laugh instead of being annoyed?"

"Stop doing that!" Mystic shouted. "I hate it when you startle me like that!"

"Okay, okay," the voice said, amused. "But before you get too angry and send me away again, let me make a suggestion: perhaps you should go and see Lili and Lulu?"

Mystic was breathing hard and couldn't respond to the voice before it was gone.

That voice is going to be the death of me, he thought grumpily.

After calming down again, Mystic thought about the advice it had given him. He'd already visited Lili and Lulu once, and they hadn't known anything about Bumpa's location, only that he had gone happily into the back of the truck—the same one that had taken the polar bears away.

As he thought, his stomach started to growl and it grew harder to concentrate.

Maybe I should pay Lili and Lulu a visit. I certainly can't stay in these dangerous woods starving to death, and maybe they'll know how I can get some food.

Food and the prospect of good company were beginning to lift his spirits, and the relief it brought with it felt amazing. He hated to admit that the wild cats, Freedom, and the voice were right, but he had to. It certainly was wonderful to feel better. All the tension in his jaw and back were letting go.

It's like that state of peacefulness I was feeling this morning. It was fantastic! At least until the voice showed up and ruined it.

But Mystic didn't want to think about it too much, because every time he did he started to lose control of himself again. The feeling of happiness (or at least of feeling better) had shown itself to be delightful on one side and dangerous on the other.

And the good feelings never last, either. When I'm feeling better, that voice always shows up and spoils everything.

Happiness was beginning to feel deceptive.

When I'm happy, I do crazy things that end up hurting me, like giving away my home. And then, when I'm not happy anymore...it's even worse! It's like happiness is a joke. It's fleeting and it's like—

"You're right!"

Mystic whirled around to face whomever had spoken. It was Trembly, approaching with a look of satisfaction.

"Happiness *is* an illusion, Mystic." Trembly came closer and sat beside Mystic. "It never lasts. And it always leaves pain behind when it goes."

Mystic said nothing. It was as if Trembly could hear what he was thinking, and Mystic didn't disagree with anything he was saying.

"Those wild cats and this voice that keeps talking inside you, they want you to believe that everything is *good*, that there's nothing wrong with anything, and that you should just focus on feeling better." Trembly laughed his muddy laugh. "And look what you did in your state of euphoria! It caused you more pain than you had before and—"

"I really enjoyed giving Tiny a home and Sarah a kitten!" Mystic said. "Tiny needed a home, and Sarah needed a friend because I was leaving to look for Bumpa. And the joy I felt that allowed me to bring them together...it was absolutely amazing. I would go through it all again to have that feeling back!"

Mystic's mouth closed with a snap, and he stared dumbfounded at Trembly. He couldn't believe the words that had just come out of his mouth. Until he had spoken them, he had no idea he even felt that way, and now here he was ready to relive the most painful few days of his entire life just to feel that happiness again.

So does that mean happiness is real? And if it is, is it really as dangerous as I thought, or is it something I should strive for?

He was deeply confused. He didn't even know what he wanted anymore. He had thought he would give anything to have his comfortable home and family back, but perhaps not. Nothing made sense anymore. What he thought he'd known for certain had changed drastically.

I need help.

"That may be what you think you'd do—" But Trembly was interrupted by heavy rustling on his left side. Startled, Mystic looked to see Freedom appear from behind the bush with an elegant leap, land beside Trembly, and delicately put her paw on his lips.

"Hush, Trembly," she whispered, a large smile on her face.

Mystic felt his heart lift a little and beat more quickly. And when he saw what she was doing to Trembly, he was impressed. She was much smaller and slenderer than Trembly, and yet the large red cat obeyed her as if she were three times his size. She had shut him down with one powerful touch. It was astonishing to witness.

"You've done enough, Trembly," she said. "*More* than enough. So just hush for now." She removed her paw from Trembly's lips. He stayed motionless and speechless, like a red, furry boulder. There was a look in his eyes that Mystic thought was annoyance, but it was fleeting, and before he could tell for sure, it was gone.

She is so powerful!

Mystic suddenly wanted to know more about Freedom and about her power. More than that, though, he wanted that power, too.

And then it hit him. Freedom had spoken of power the last time they had met.

Could this be what she was referring to? If I keep practicing feeling better, will I be able to wield that power, too?

Freedom was still speaking to Trembly, who was sitting and listening to her the way Sarah would sometimes sit and listen to Jean and Pete when they were explaining something serious.

"Why don't you go to the top of that hill over there and see if you can find me? If I'm not there, wait for me," she said, motioning him away with a lazy flap of her paw.

"Trying to send someone else on a fool's errand, are you?" Trembly said and turned to look at Mystic. "At least I *know* it's a fool's errand." Mystic could hear the irritation in his voice, though. He was sure that Freedom heard it, too, but if she had, she made no indication.

"There's plenty of other prey out there, Trembly," she said as he began to stalk away. "Mystic's point of view is already beginning to change. It's too late for you."

Trembly looked back at her with a wide, false smile. "That's your opinion," he said. Then he disappeared into the bushes, leaving Freedom and Mystic alone in the clearing.

-3-

As Freedom faced Mystic, he was already asking the

questions that had flooded his mind when he'd watched her interaction with Trembly. His mouth was going a mile a minute. "How did you do that—make him feel so weak? He didn't even try to fight back! What happened? And why did you tell him I wasn't prey anymore and that my point of view had changed? And why would I be prey anyway?"

"Oh wow, that's a whole lot of questions." Freedom laughed. "Relax. Take a breath!" She placed her front paws on Mystic's shoulders. "You know, you're kind of cute when you're excited."

Her touch captured his attention at once. He felt sudden calm spreading throughout his body. "How do you do that?" he whispered, glancing at her paw on his shoulder.

"I'm not doing anything." She dropped down to all fours again. "I'm just feeling as good as I can, and I trust that what I want is happening. I trust life in a way that others would probably say was crazy or even wrong."

"You sound like you're speaking squirrel," Mystic said, laughing a little.

Freedom giggled. "I've practiced talking about and looking for things that make me feel good. Or at least, things that don't cause any negative feelings. It can be anything at all in the whole world. Doing this has allowed me to perceive only that which brings me joy…and let me tell you, Mystic, it's so effective…it's powerful!" Freedom looked once more as if she was watching a pleasant memory that only she could see.

"I guess, I understand the basic idea," Mystic said slowly.

"Good! That's the first step!"

He shook his head. "But I still don't know how it all works."

"Don't worry about that for now. Just concentrate on the idea. Practice it. And, in time, you'll understand it fully…but *only* if you practice."

"So just focus on and talk about what feels good?" Mystic said. He still wasn't convinced that it would actually work.

"Yes!"

"But I don't want to practice anything! The last time I tried that, I made a terrible mistake and—"

"Your action only became a mistake in your eyes the moment you started to listen to your fears," Freedom said. "Think back and you'll know it's true."

Mystic did and discovered that Freedom was right. Everything had been going so smoothly until he had a negative thought about how to find Bumpa. Then everything had collapsed.

"At that moment, you stopped trusting everything and everyone, didn't you? Even yourself and your decisions?"

Mystic nodded.

"When you were focused on feeling better, everything was easy. And you got such joy from taking Tiny to your home and introducing him to Sarah, don't you remember? What you think of now as your mistake gave you a tremendous feeling of joy at the time."

Mystic thought of the scene again and felt moved by it. "I was very emotional, and yes, the strongest feeling was joy. I was happy for Tiny and Sarah."

"And the moment you let fear invade your thinking, this

blissful emotion changed," Freedom said more quietly.

Mystic remembered the terror he had felt just after he realized he had no idea how to find Bumpa. "But I had reasons to be scared."

"I agree," Freedom said softly. "But then your fear took you down endlessly until you were losing yourself in an abyss of despair. Even now you're not entirely free from it."

Mystic had been pleased when Freedom had agreed with him, but the feeling was short-lived. Still, he was intrigued and wanted to know more.

"It's okay to get scared or hurt," she continued. "It's normal to experience those emotions. I experience them myself; everyone does at some point."

It was hard for Mystic to picture Freedom hurt or afraid. She possessed so much strength that it didn't seem possible. He was burning with curiosity to know exactly what could make such a brave cat afraid, but he knew now was not the time to talk about it.

Freedom came over to where Mystic sat and nudged him softly with her head. "The trick, though, is not letting those negative emotions drag you down. Because they'll grab a hold of you and shake you like a wolf will a lamb and refuse to let go. The only way to escape their grip is by changing what you focus on. *You* need to be the stronger one, Mystic, and *you* need to be the one to let go of the negativity."

With that, it became clear in Mystic's mind. "Trembly," he stammered, "Trembly's the fear, and I'm his prey."

"Yes, that's right," Freedom said. "Well, at least you were his prey, but not anymore. Your mind is beginning to change. You admitted that feeling good is wonderful, and you even said that you would go through everything you have in the last few days to experience the joy you felt again, didn't you?"

"Yes, I did," Mystic said. "But I hate to admit that you and those crazy cats are right."

Freedom only giggled.

"So, if Trembly is fear, are you his opposite?"

Freedom smiled. "No, Mystic, I'm just a cat like you and all the others. I like to help; it's what gives me joy."

"So, who is Trembly's opposite? Is it one of the cats in the park?"

"No, it's not a cat in the park. In fact, it doesn't exist outside you at all. There is an opposite to Trembly—to that fear emotion you experience—but it exists within you."

At those words Mystic was reminded that the voice had said it came from within.

No, no, no, he thought. *That thing is annoying and nasty. All it wants is to ruin my happy time. It can't be that...*

"Trembly's opposite, the opposite of your fear," Freedom said, "is the voice inside you that shows up whenever you allow it to come."

"No!" Mystic grumbled. "It can't be. I don't want that to be it!"

Freedom laughed.

"That voice is nasty! It shows up out of nowhere and scares me every time! It destroys my good mood each time I start to feel a little bit better, and it laughs at me! It has no compassion whatsoever!"

"It can only come to you when you allow it to. When your emotional state will let it come."

"No, no, no!" Mystic shouted. "I never let it come! It just shows up whenever it wants to! Believe me, if I could control it, I would never hear from it ever again!"

"For now you're doing it unconsciously," Freedom said. "Whenever you feel relief from negative emotions, you give it permission. It can't show up when you're angry or depressed."

"Well, I hate it." Mystic wasn't ready to concede this point yet. He was getting fed-up with the subject in general.

"You don't hate it, Mystic. You're just not used to it, that's all. But trust me, it really is a happy part of you, and it knows everything you need to have an incredible life."

"Well, why can't it be *you* instead of this voice in my head? Why can't it be a nice cat like you?"

"Because wellbeing is a part of who you are, and it's different for everyone," she said. "It can't come from the outside; it *has* to come from within you. It's your intuition, and it's not always a voice. Sometimes it's a strong urge or idea that you should do something. Sometimes it comes as images and you see yourself doing something that will bring you great joy. Yours is a voice now because that's what you need now. Fear on the other hand, just like any negative emotion, isn't a part of you, but rather something you pick up from the outside. It could be caused by something that happens or someone else's beliefs, but it's not who you are."

Mystic felt more confused than ever.

He sighed. He was tired and wanted to eat, but before he could do anything else, there was another question he had to know the answer to.

"Why were you so nice to Trembly?"

"Because kindness, joy...any positive feeling...that's what's powerful, Mystic."

"But why does he even have to exist? What's the point?"

"Sometimes a cat like you will have to experience pain and fear in order to grow and change their way of thinking," she said. "Trembly's purpose is to see that you do, but there's no malice in what he does. He is a necessary part of the process for some, and therefore important. He helps them."

"I refuse to believe that!"

"That's fine, Mystic, you don't have to. What I've just told you is just information, and you decide whether to listen to it or not. And whatever you choose to believe will become your truth."

Mystic opened his mouth to protest again, but Freedom spoke before he could.

"Just don't worry about understanding or even remembering everything all at once. As you go through life, understanding will gradually come to you, and you'll be surprised by what you remember. For now, just trust that all is good."

"But what if it hurts?" Mystic worried. "Giving my home away hurt as much as it gave me joy!"

"You can choose to believe your fear, and that it will hurt. Or you can choose to believe your happiness, and that it will be gratifying."

Mystic just stared at her. His brain felt cooked. He was surprised he was still standing upright.

Freedom giggled. "You look tired. You should go to Lili and Lulu now. They should be able to help you find some food."

Mystic stared at the unfamiliar trees and paths around him. "I don't even know where I am anymore."

"Just go straight this way." Freedom nodded her head to the right. She turned to the left and ran a little way down a path between two trees. As she did, Mystic felt a sharp pain in his chest.

"Wait! Hey wait!" he called after her.

She stopped and turned back with a smile. "Yes, Mystic?"

"Can't you stay with me longer? Or come with me to see Lili and Lulu? When you leave me, it hurts."

"I really like you, Mystic," Freedom said, and Mystic beamed. "But it's not my absence that hurts you. You're missing the way you feel when we're together. And it's the same with Bumpa. You should focus on finding a way to capture that feeling so you can experience it when we're not together." She had walked back toward him as she spoke, and now she was standing close. "It's what I do," she added, leaning in and kissing him gently on the cheek. "You'll see, it will set you free," she whispered and, with a smile, bounded away down her path, leaving Mystic staring after her.

His cheek was still tingling from where she had kissed him, and all the confusion that had felt so heavy only moments before was now much lighter. *I'm going to do it,* he thought. *And I'll make her proud of me, and then she'll come back.* He had no idea exactly *how* he would do it, but that didn't matter.

What did matter now was getting some food. Mystic spared one last glance for the path Freedom had taken and turned to the path she had pointed out to him. He walked briskly, and before he knew it, he was running.

Lulu

6

Lili

A CHANGE IN PERCEPTION

-1-

Mystic had only been running for a short time before he started to recognize the area around him. He hadn't been all that far from the enclosures after all.

It was because I panicked that everything looked so alien, he thought. *Next time I'll try to stay calmer.*

The park was quiet, and Mystic was glad of that. If it had been crowded with people, the situation would have been more difficult. As it was, he could move along with no trouble at all.

Freedom must have given me some good luck, he thought and smiled. He was heading down the paved path toward the giraffe's enclosure, when he heard someone calling to him. He was surprised to see Lulu's head towering over the top of a nearby wall.

"You look rather happy today," Lulu said.

"You've been moved!"

"Yes!" Lulu said enthusiastically, waving his long neck. "Isn't it fantastic? There're more trees, more room to move around, and even more visitors. We're almost at the center of the park here, and everyone passes by this spot."

Lili came up behind him, grinning from ear to ear. "Can you believe you didn't even see me?" she said. "This place is so big that you can't see the whole thing from where you're standing!"

"We like to play with the visitors," Lulu giggled. "When they approach, we hide in the trees on the other side, and they walk by without even seeing us! It's hilarious!"

Mystic was dazzled by their moods. They had always been upbeat, but now the giraffes were positively giddy. "It's so great to see you like this. Really!"

After what Mystic had gone through last night and then again this morning with the voice and Trembly, it felt wonderful to see Lulu doubled over, shaking with laughter. Their happiness was infectious, but it didn't stop him from feeling starved.

"I met Freedom, and she said you could probably help me get some food," he said.

"Well, you're in luck." Lili nodded over to the corner. "This pen is where they used to keep the lions, and there's still some meat left on the side over there." She stuck out her tongue and made an exaggerated choking sound. "It's disgusting. But please, help yourself. I'm glad Freedom remembered it was here!"

Mystic was so excited there was food nearby that he didn't say a word. He scrambled into the enclosure, ran to the corner, and found the pile of meat. It wasn't really fresh and was a little hard to chew, but the flavor was beyond anything he'd had since leaving home. He ate with great relish.

Once his belly was full, he wandered over to where Lili and Lulu were looking down at him with distaste.

"Absolutely delicious!" he teased them, licking the last bits of meat out of his whiskers.

"Yuck," Lulu shuddered and scrunched his face up as if the meat had actually touched his tongue.

"Well, we're glad Freedom told you about it," Lili said. "The sooner it's gone, the better."

"I'm glad she told me, too. I was starving." Mystic washed his paws and face while Lili and Lulu grazed, then a thought occurred to him. "Do you know Freedom well?"

"Yes, she often comes and talks with us," Lulu said.

"We're friends," Lili added.

"I wish she came and saw *me* that often."

"What's that?" Lulu said, his voice teasing. "What's going on here?"

"No, it's not what you think." Mystic's cheeks were burning red under his fur. "I just really enjoy having her beside me. She makes me feel...I don't know, important I guess. Like I'm strong and worthy and safe..."

"And alive!" Lili added.

"Yes, that's it!" Mystic said. "Alive...all of it added up, that's how she makes me feel."

The three were silent for a moment, their eyes dreamy and faraway as if watching some wonderful memory. No one said a word until the moment was broken by the rusty cry of a crow in a nearby tree.

"Did Freedom tell you to try and achieve that feeling when she wasn't around?" Mystic asked.

"Yes," Lili and Lulu replied at the same time.

"And we've just done it, haven't we?" Lulu added with a look of satisfaction.

"Yes, I guess we did," Mystic said, but the feeling was dissipating rapidly. "But *how* did we do that?" He couldn't remember exactly how they had gotten there.

"We just brought back the memory of it," Lili said. "It's obvious, isn't it?"

"Not to me." Mystic slumped down to the dirt, feeling like a total failure. "To me it feels like *nothing* is obvious. Nothing is as simple for me as it is for you. It's as if I was born with something missing. Apparently, there are many things I don't know and don't understand."

"It's okay, Mystic," Lulu said softly. "You know, Freedom was like you when she was a kitten, and just look at her now."

Mystic stood and look at the giraffes with surprise. "Really? She was like me?"

Lulu nodded and smiled.

"Everybody knows it," Lili added. "We never heard her say it directly, but then again we've never asked her either. But everyone says it, and we believe it's true."

Mystic felt a sudden wave of hopefulness. When Freedom had told him he could reach her power, she knew what she was talking about because she had actually done it.

"Wow," he said under his breath, amazed by this new bit of information. The giraffes looked at him with amused smiles.

"So what did Freedom say to *you*?" Lulu asked eagerly.

"I think...I think she said that, if I practiced looking for ways to feel good, I could reach the power that she has to control fear." Mystic thought back to the way Freedom had silenced and then banished Trembly. "Do you guys have that power, too?"

"Yes," Lili said, "but it's sorta difficult to explain how

to reach it. It's something that occurs naturally within us. We don't even have to think about it, it just happens."

"So, how do you know you have it then?"

"Because when we get afraid, it doesn't consume us," Lulu said.

"And unlike Freedom, we don't have to make a conscious effort to push it away," Lili said. "It happens without us knowing. It's just a moment of fear, sometimes panic, or aggressiveness, and then it's gone as if nothing ever happened."

Mystic was suddenly annoyed. "How is that fair? Why is it that you received this gift without having to work for it, and I have to work and struggle so hard? Is it because I'm less than you or not worthy enough?"

"Who said you were less than us or unworthy just because you're different?" Lulu said. "There's nothing wrong with being different."

"It just feels that way!" Mystic shouted more sharply than he had intended. It was so frustrating that he wasn't able to articulate exactly how it felt to live in his skin and to watch others move around with such carefree attitudes all the time.

"It may feel that way, Mystic, but it isn't that way," Lulu said.

Lili Nodded. "Besides, with all your negativity, you're missing the best part."

"And what's that?" Mystic didn't know what could possibly be good about this situation.

"You've already forgotten what we said about you and Freedom being the same," she said. "You're so attached to your negativity, you're dismissing all the positivity that also goes along with it."

"I don't see anything positive in having to learn what I could have known from the start."

"Well, don't you think that, because she had to learn how to control fear, she might be able to teach you how to do it better?"

"And just maybe, her power would be even stronger than ours because she had to work so hard to attain it," Lulu added.

"And that maybe *your* power could become equally strong because you have to learn it, too?" Lili said.

Mystic was quiet for a moment considering this, and as he did he felt a faint glimmer of hope. If what they were saying was true—and why would they lie to him?—then he might one day have power equal to Freedom's. It was a seductive thought.

"You'd be wise to listen to her, Mystic," Lulu said, taking a mouthful of leaves and chewing them slowly. "She has power beyond even what we do. Don't tell me you haven't noticed that before."

Mystic recalled how she had appeased him with only a touch from her paw, and the intense calm that had flooded through him. He shuddered. If what they were saying was right, what he had seen as a defect in himself might actually be a huge advantage. It was hard to believe, but he desperately wanted to.

"She may push you a little bit more than you'd like, Mystic, but it's because she sees greatness within you," Lili said, joining Lulu in a snack of acacia leaves.

Mystic wandered back over to the meat to pick at it a

little more, but he wasn't really hungry. Everything Lili and Lulu had told him was going through his mind, and he was trying to process it.

As he sat there thinking, an image came to him as clear as polished glass. It was of Bumpa sitting on his wooden platform, looking up at a sky full of shooting stars. Mystic stood and wandered back over to where Lili and Lulu were grazing.

They didn't see him at first, so he cleared his throat and they bent down, still contentedly munching on their leaves.

"Do you...do you think I can find Bumpa?" he asked, a little embarrassed.

"Why wouldn't you be able to?" Lili said.

"Because when I try to picture where he is now, what his new enclosure might look like, what he might be doing, I see nothing," Mystic said in a small sad voice. "I'm totally clueless as to what to do or even where to begin looking."

"Have you been listening to your intuition?" Lili asked, and Mystic scrunched his face up.

"Ugh, Freedom told me about my intuition," he said. "I can't stand that voice."

Lili laughed quietly. "I remember Freedom saying that it was hard for her to listen to at first, but the more she did, the easier it got. You know how to call it, don't you?"

"Apparently, when I'm feeling better or relieved I give it permission to come. But I wouldn't even know how I could feel better right now. Nothing is right at all."

"Are you sick?" Lulu asked.

"What? No, I'm not sick."

"And didn't you have a nice filling lunch and delightful

company here with us today?" Lili said.

"Yes, I guess I did." Mystic thought about the taste of the meat and the warm full feeling he had immediately after eating.

"Well, those are all positive things, aren't they?" Lulu said. "Positive things and things you should be focusing on instead of all you think is going wrong."

"I guess so."

"What made you come here in the first place?" Lili asked suddenly.

Mystic thought for a moment. "Well, Freedom told me to come here and that you might know where I could get some food." But as soon as the words were out of his mouth, he knew they were wrong. "Actually, she told me to come here only *after* the voice had told me I should. It told me to come here and talk to you. I'd forgotten about that until now."

"You see!" Lili said. "This was your intuition. It's there to help you! Listen to it, and I bet you'll find Bumpa in no time at all!"

Could Lili be right? he wondered. *Could that annoying little pipsqueak of a voice in my head really help me find Bumpa?* It had given him good advice, after all, and it only showed up when he was feeling better about himself. *And what if that voice had known that Lili and Lulu would tell me all about how Freedom used to be?* He was becoming more excited. Maybe—just maybe—the next time it spoke up, he would listen to what it had to say before trying to send it away.

There was a clattering at the gate. Lili and Lulu turned immediately toward it.

"We have to go," Lili said, and without another word, the two trotted toward the sound.

A young woman with curly red hair stood by the door, holding a white bucket in her hand full of carrots and small brown biscuits. She looked very kind to Mystic, and for a moment he could almost see Sarah in her face.

The woman looked happy to see them approaching the gate and smiled, saying something that Mystic couldn't hear. When Lili and Lulu were closer, she tipped the bucket over on the ground and scattered the goodies out. Lulu dipped his head and began to eat, while Lili went to greet the woman, who scratched the end of Lili's nose affectionately.

Mystic turned away from them, allowing them their privacy. He lay out in a patch of sunlight, his stomach swelled with food, his fur warm. As he was relaxing, he thought about today's discoveries and what they might mean.

Can I really believe all of this? I don't feel any more powerful now than I did before, and when the voice-intuition thing shows up, I don't even have any idea what to do with it.

The hope he had been feeling only moments ago was clouded by his doubt, and even relaxing in the sun as he was, Mystic began to tense up again. *It just sounds too good to be true.*

"Doesn't it?" Trembly said suddenly from in front of

him. Mystic hadn't seen him approaching; he was just there, smiling coyly to himself and twitching his tail back and forth.

"Not you again!"

"And why not me again?"

"Don't try to intimidate me, *Mister* Trembly," Mystic sneered. "I saw you with Freedom this morning, and you can just climb down off your high horse. I saw the way she put you in your place."

Incredibly, Trembly laughed at him, and Mystic's face collapsed a little. "Don't think you're impressing me, Mystic. Far from it, actually. Freedom may have sent me away this morning, but I'm feeling much, *much* stronger now, and it looks like you're the same scared little cat you always were." He smiled a loathsome smile that reminded Mystic of a snake. It was then he noticed that Trembly's eye, the green one, was much darker than it had been before.

Maybe that's just a trick of the light.

But the longer Mystic looked, the more he thought that, no, Trembly's green eye was almost black. A shiver ran up his spine. He tried to suppress it but couldn't quite, and Trembly laughed again when he saw it.

All Mystic's bravado fell away. He felt vulnerable and in danger once again. He couldn't help it. What he had discussed with Lili and Lulu was far from his mind. He felt like he was falling down an endless well of terror and pain.

If I can't even handle this now, I'll never succeed in achieving any power.

The world was spinning around him, his chest heavy with despair. The pain that came to him now was worse than anything he had experienced so far, the fear of being unworthy, of never experiencing a good life again or finding happiness. The fear of losing Freedom. This last especially felt like someone had shot an arrow through his chest. All the hope he had of being someone special and powerful was gone.

Mystic looked up for an escape route—he couldn't stand to sit here anymore and listen to what that horrible red cat was saying—but his eyes met Trembly's and he froze. Trembly was puffed up and looked larger than he had before, his face disfigured by a smile of twisted delight. Mystic was humiliated that he had even thought he could be like Freedom. What a joke that was.

I'm weak, I'm a loser, he thought miserably. He fell to the ground, his head between his front paws and his eyes clenched shut.

"Please just go away," he begged.

Trembly chuckled. He sounded only inches away from Mystic's head, as if he had slithered closer when Mystic wasn't looking. When Trembly spoke, his voice was low and deadly. "You see where false hope and delusions will get you? They only lead to more suffering."

"Please," Mystic begged again, his voice muffled by his front paws. "Stop. Just leave me alone."

"Did you really believe you were special?" Trembly asked with a nasty laugh. "That your intuition would somehow help you in this life? Well, where is it? Why don't you call it?"

"I can't," Mystic whispered, humiliated.

"Of course you can't," Trembly said, his voice full of

disgust. "Everything they've said has been a lie. You're alone in this unfriendly world, Mystic. You're *alone*." His breath tickled the hair in Mystic's ears, and he almost screamed.

"And even if what they told you was the truth, you'd never find a way to achieve it," Trembly hissed. "You could never find a way to become like them, and you'd have even *less* of a chance of becoming like Freedom. You don't deserve it and you never did."

His words were like knives piercing Mystic's heart, each one bleeding out a little more of the life from within him. He was drowning in pain.

Trembly was right. He wasn't as worthy as the others. He wasn't strong enough to work as hard as Freedom had to achieve her power and her joy. Happiness wasn't for him.

-*3*-

Mystic was overtaken by a tremendous need to just run away.

Why aren't Lili and Lulu doing anything to help me? They had been just behind him only a moment before, eating and visiting with their caretaker. They must have seen Trembly. But he couldn't even hear them anymore; all was silent except for his own ragged breath. *They left me,* he thought miserably. *They left me, and I really am all alone.*

Knowing they were gone made him want them all the more—he needed their love and the comfort and safety they provided—so despite his fear, he decided to take a chance and look for them. He removed one paw from his head.

Waited a moment to see if Trembly would speak. When he didn't, Mystic removed his other paw. His eyes still scrunched shut, he took a deep breath and prepared to open them, terrified that Trembly's horrific face would be inches from his own.

When he had mustered as much courage as he could, he peered through the slits between his eyelashes.

Trembly was no longer there. *That doesn't mean he's gone, though.* Mystic chanced turning his head to the left and right to spy the gaudy red of Trembly's fur. But he was gone. Mystic opened his eyes fully and blinked a few times in disbelief.

He turned, hoping to see Lili and Lulu behind him, still contentedly munching away at their lunch, but he stopped dead and stared at the empty enclosure.

Terror flooded his body. *Trembly was right! He said I was alone, and I am. I'm alone! I'm alone!* His heart beat wildly, his throat cinched so tight he couldn't breathe.

NO! No, no, NO! They can't be gone! They have to be here somewhere! He spun in a circle and looked for them, sure he would see their heads towering over the low-lying plants at any moment, but soon he was back to the gate and hadn't seen them at all. *Did someone come and take them like they took Bumpa?* he thought frantically. *Were they moved to another place?* It made no sense. He hadn't heard a truck coming or people talking, but then Trembly had been commanding all his attention, so he could easily see how he would have missed that.

I must catch them before they're gone. Without hesitation, he scrambled up the wall and out of the enclosure.

There weren't many people at the park, and Mystic ran down the path without interference. Cages passed by in a blur, and he ignored them. They were much too small for the giraffes anyway. Then up ahead he spied one that could be large enough. It was where the ostriches had lived until they moved to a larger enclosure with a bigger pasture. He turned toward it and ran, but before he made it, a large colorful bird flew toward him. Mystic was immediately transported back to the previous night in the woods when the large screeching bird had attacked him. He screamed as if it were angling for his eyes. The bird landed on the path a few feet away and cocked its head quizzically to the side. It uttered a short hoot and hopped away into the bushes on the other side of the path.

Mystic stumbled back from the bird, crashed through the flowers lining the path, before sliding down a short hill and through the bars of another cage. He landed on his back, breathing heavily, his fur covered in dead leaves and clumps of dirt.

Could today get any worse? He was staring at the top of the cage and, beyond it, at the blue sky when a dark shape hurtled toward him from one of the stunted little bushes to the right. With it came a high-pitched screeching.

"WHAT ARE YOU DOING HERE?" it said, and before Mystic could answer, the dark shape landed on top of him, momentarily knocking the wind out of him. Hands clasped his front paws, restraining them and pushing them down to the dirt.

Mystic dared look up and found himself staring into the face of a muscular blonde monkey, who was sitting on his chest. The monkey looked in rough shape; his fur was patchy and missing in places, revealing pink skin below. Deep round scars covered his head. He looked terrifying.

The monkey bared his teeth at Mystic, making a low hissing in the back of his throat. "Why are you teasing those of us who aren't free?" he growled. "You don't know what it's like to be jailed here, or you would never do what you're doing."

"I can't breathe," Mystic wheezed, noticing black dots blossoming before his eyes. There was a moment more of pressure, then it was gone and he could breathe again. He dragged in a few shaky breaths and coughed.

The monkey sat beside him, still holding Mystic's paws down, but no longer baring his teeth or hissing.

"I'm sorry," Mystic managed to say. He had never thought of the park as a place that lacked freedom before, but he supposed that, to some of the animals, it must feel that way. He could come and go as he pleased, but not many could. He felt a momentary embarrassment. "I'm sorry," he whispered again.

The monkey looked at him with frustration and, with a snort, released Mystic's paws. Mystic could barely move his toes—the monkey had squeezed his paws very strongly— but as he flexed them, feeling slowly began to return. With it came shame.

"I really am sorry." Mystic felt foolish, but it was all he could think to say.

"It's fine, it's not your fault." The monkey's cloudy eyes revealed weariness. "You didn't realize what you were doing." He was beginning to calm down, and Mystic's fear slowly subsided.

"I should have, though…I'm just…just stupid, just a lost cause." All the emotions from his encounter with Trembly were returning, combined with his new sense of shame from his ignorance. He sighed with disgust.

"Go on, get out of here, kid." The monkey turned and stepped away from Mystic, dragging his feet on the ground as if they weighed a thousand pounds, his shoulders slumped and his head hung low.

He looks as depressed as I feel.

"Why are you here by yourself?" Mystic blurted out before he even realized he was speaking. Immediately, he regretted it. He was certain the monkey would turn and start screaming and shrieking (and maybe even jump back onto his chest), but he didn't. He just kept shuffling, his shoulders still slumped.

"I used to have a mate, but she died," he said.

Mystic felt his skin flush redder than it ever had before. He was sure his fur must be glowing pink with embarrassment. "I—I'm so—"

"Don't worry about me, kid, I'll be okay." The monkey disappeared into the bushes without so much as a glance back.

Mystic was in shock from everything that had happened, and for a moment he just lay in the dirt. The terror he'd experienced with Trembly and then when the monkey had appeared was second now to his feeling of sadness. But now was not the time to dwell on that. He wanted to be gone before the monkey returned and got mad at him all over again for still being there.

126

He stood and headed back to the enclosure where he had last seen Lili and Lulu. In his panic he had neglected to search very well; maybe if he returned, he would find some clues as to where they had gone.

-4-

Before Lili and Lulu's enclosure was even in sight, Mystic heard something he hadn't expected. It was Lulu's voice.

He started to run and then leapt up onto the wall. Lulu was humming as he groomed Lili's back with his long tongue.

"There you are!" Lulu said, looking up and catching Mystic's eye. "I saw you running away and called you, but you"

"Where were you?" Mystic shouted. "I was just here and I looked and looked for you, but you were gone!"

"Lower your voice," Lili said, and Mystic was a little unnerved by her reproach. He'd never heard her speak like that to anyone before. "Now what in the world are you talking about?"

"I was in trouble! In danger! And you didn't do anything to help me! You just disappeared!"

"We've been here the whole time, Mystic, and we saw nothing dangerous," Lulu said.

"We don't know what you're talking about," Lili added.

Mystic sat down hard on the ground, his tail limp and lifeless, his ears drooping. He felt so misunderstood and betrayed. The weight of all this negativity was pushing him down.

"Hey, hey, hey, it's all right."

Mystic's ears perked up at the sound of the voice. He recognized it instantly. It was Freedom. She was atop the wall opposite him, approaching from behind Lili and Lulu.

"They *were* right here, Mystic. No one betrayed you."

"Ah, Freedom," Lili said with relief. "You always have such perfect timing."

Mystic watched her but said nothing. He had said far too many idiotic things in the last few days, and he didn't want to add to them. If Freedom was here, it meant she was going to explain something, so he decided to just wait.

She leapt from the low wall to a rock inside Lili and Lulu's enclosure and then picked her way carefully down from rock to rock until she was standing close to the giraffes. Mystic was absorbed by the image of her lithe body moving so elegantly. Most cats moved with grace, but Freedom was beyond graceful.

She stopped on a large flat rock at the same height as the giraffe's heads, and they spoke easily with one another.

"What's going on?" Lulu asked Freedom.

"I believe it's our good friend Trembly," Freedom said, looking up at Mystic for corroboration. He nodded.

"Oh no!" Lili and Lulu exclaimed at the same time, eyeing Mystic with compassion.

"Poor thing," Lili said.

"You really didn't see him?"

"No, we didn't."

"But he was here! Right over there!" Mystic insisted, indicating the patch of ground where he had been lounging when Trembly had shown up.

"Maybe we were inside drinking," Lulu shrugged.

"At the exact time that Trembly showed up? That's a little hard to believe, isn't it?"

"It's just bad luck, Mystic," Lulu said. "When I came out from getting a drink, I saw you running away and called to you, but you didn't see me or hear me, and you just kept running."

Mystic shook his head in disbelief. "But I looked for you before that! You weren't here, and I thought that maybe they'd moved you to another pen—that's where I was going! I never heard you call me at all!" He was out of breath. The entire situation was incomprehensible.

"Well, you didn't find us anywhere else, did you?" Lili asked.

"No, of course not," Mystic said, giving in a little. He knew they had to be right, that they'd been here all along. He had just not seen them. But still, he didn't understand how he had missed them entirely. He turned to Freedom and asked her to explain it.

Lili and Lulu turned in tandem to her too, and she burst out laughing.

"I'm not saying anything," she said. "I don't have to, because I've said it before. Think, Mystic."

Mystic knew he would never sway her, that he would have to figure it out. It was a part of what Lili and Lulu had talked about earlier with the learning process, but that didn't make it any less frustrating.

But this time, before the frustration could grow and overtake him, he decided to calm down and think. *I need to find the answer while she's still here. I don't want to lose this opportunity.*

He took a few deep breaths and organized his thoughts. When he finally did, he spoke slowly. "You told me they were in their pen the entire time, but I couldn't see them." Freedom was smiling and nodding. "But why? Why couldn't I see them when they were right in front of me like Lulu said?"

"Why don't you come down here and join us?" Freedom said. "Being a part of a group instead of all alone might help you figure it out."

Mystic started down the wall without hesitation. There was something wonderful about being invited to be a part of a group, especially one which contained Freedom. He was no longer feeling quite like the outsider he had before, and his spirits were beginning to lift when he stopped on a large warm rock.

It's going to come, Mystic thought with certainty. *That voice, my intuition, it's going to come now. I'm feeling better than I was, and if I ever had a need for it, it's now. I'm certain it will come.*

"Did you miss me?" the voice asked, and this time, prepared for it, Mystic didn't jump. He noticed Freedom, Lili and Lulu watching him from below, smiling patiently.

He was trying not to be overly cross with the voice, but it was difficult. He thought that if it stayed for only a short time, he was less likely to get angry at it and lose his good mood entirely, so said "I need your help. And once I have it, you can go."

"I know what you need," the voice said. "And this is

what I can tell you. Whatever you think, you will feel, hear, and see."

"That's it?" Mystic was annoyed despite his effort.

But the voice didn't respond. It had given its advice and then retreated like he'd told it to.

"Come down, Mystic," Freedom said. "Come tell us what your intuition told you."

Mystic, no longer surprised that Freedom was so in tune with what was happening within him, hopped down the last few boulders until he was beside her on the large flat rock.

"It was something like, 'What I think is what I feel, hear, and see,'" he replied.

"And do you understand what it means?"

"I think so, but I'm not sure," he said. "All these new emotions and feelings coming so close to the terror of Trembly...It's a lot."

"Just tell me what you think it means then."

"I think it has to do with Trembly," he started, gathering his thoughts once again. "When he told me I was all alone, I must have believed him, and because of that, I couldn't see Lulu when he was right in front of me."

Freedom nodded but said nothing. Reassured, Mystic went on.

"And then I felt I was in great danger. Trembly's appearance had changed, and he was much more menacing this time...and that's why I only encountered the bird and then the monkey...things that were scary instead of pleasant."

Freedom was nodding more vigorously now but still said nothing.

"That's why you and the wild cats are always telling me to find ways to think positively and feel good, isn't it?" He was hoping that Freedom would scream "Yes!" and say "You've done it!" but she wasn't even nodding anymore. She wore a large smile but wasn't moving a muscle.

Mystic had no choice but to charge ahead and finish his thought without help. It was a little scary, but it was also exhilarating.

"Because if I find ways to think positively and trust that everything is fine, I will actually start to feel good and perceive things in a positive way. Like, I wouldn't have been spooked by that bird earlier…or the monkey. In fact, if I learn to think positively, maybe the monkey wouldn't even scare me at all anymore. That's it, isn't it?"

He hoped that Freedom would react this time because he didn't know what else to add. And she did. She jumped up and flung her arms around his neck in a hug.

"What a phenomenal leap forward into a newer happier life!" she said. "I see you as a whole different cat! I can feel your power growing, just below your skin, waiting for the moment when your life blossoms!"

Mystic only heard a little of what Freedom said to him. Her touch had quickened his heartbeat, and his skin had flushed with heat beneath his fur. Freedom was happy, she admired him, and that was all in the world he wanted. He made up his mind to work even harder at getting better and impress her more and more. The idea, coupled with her touch, was intoxicating, and he wished they could stay locked in their embrace forever.

Freedom finally stepped back. "I'm really proud of you."

Her eyes shone with pride, and Mystic was glued to them, delighted. "But I must go now. As you know, other students of happiness need me."

Once she left Mystic felt troubled, not so much by her departure, but by what she had said.

I want more than being a 'student' to her or a 'project' she works on, he thought. *And the only way to be more than that is to become more like her and prove myself to her.*

He looked at the giraffes, "I will return to the woods tonight."

"What? Why?" Lulu said.

"To show Freedom I can overcome my fears now—as she does." Mystic was eager to leave and bounced on the spot.

"You should wait," Lili said softly, as if trying to calm him. "You should practice in some less frightening situations first."

"Yes," Lulu said. "And only increase the degree of fright *very* gradually."

"Thank you for your concerns," Mystic said, "but I will go tonight." He so wanted to impress Freedom. It energized him and nothing and no one could stop him.

7

A DEEP DIVE INTO DARKNESS

1

The rest of the day went peacefully. Mystic finished his meat, enjoyed chatting with Lili and Lulu (who had stopped trying to discourage his brave, but misguided plan), and dozed in the sun until dusk finally approached. He left the giraffes behind and walked with determination in the direction of the woods.

As he went along, he decided to practice breathing deeply to ward off the negative thoughts trying to crowd their way back in. He was confident that, once darkness fell, he would be able to successfully face whatever might scare him in the night. He still felt his power that Freedom had spoken of just beneath his skin. He just needed to breathe and stay calm, and everything would work out smoothly.

But once the sun fell further below the trees and the shadows crept out of the undergrowth, Mystic discovered it wasn't as easy as he had anticipated. Memories of last night bubbled up in his mind—the bird that had tried to have him for supper, the way the trees had looked like frightening creatures reaching out to grab him, and of course, Trembly— and before he had gone too far, Mystic was shivering.

He stopped and took great gasping breaths, pulling air in through his nose and then blowing it out through his mouth, over and over. He was making too much noise, he knew that, but he didn't seem to be able to stop. His breaths were coming on their own now, and he couldn't even slow them down. His breathing was too rapid; his head started to spin. *I'm going to faint. Why isn't this working? It's worked every other time!*

The woods were whirling around him. He looked up into the overarching branches of the trees, trying to force himself to see them as beautiful, as he usually did, but those too had been commandeered by his fear. They weren't as frightening as they had been last night (none of them had moved to grab him yet), but they looked high, dark, and imposing, as if they might at any moment. It didn't matter where he looked, everything had taken on a dark and sinister cast.

He heard a rustling in front of him, and before he could even think to turn tail and run, Trembly stood before him on the path, smiling his unpleasant smile. Mystic's throat locked, and no air entered his lungs at all.

"Don't forget to breathe, Mystic, or you'll spoil all my fun," Trembly said with a piercing scream of a laugh.

The initial shock and fright that had overtaken him when Trembly appeared was diminishing. Mystic's throat relaxed enough for him to take in a few ragged breaths. Once he could breathe again, he discovered that he could think more clearly, and his conversation with Freedom began to return to him. She had shown him he could unravel Trembly's power. It had been his own lack of confidence in going into the woods that had allowed Trembly the power to step back into his life so easily.

This understanding gave Mystic even more hope, and his terror decreased. He knew that, if he kept practicing control of his emotions, he would gain even more power over Trembly. *Like Freedom has!* he thought. Conjuring up the image of Freedom, cool and in control, gave him more strength.

"I can do this," he whispered to himself.

"You can do *what*?" Trembly asked snidely, but Mystic thought he had glimpsed a faint glimmer of annoyance on the red cat's face.

He's feeling his power weakening. My understanding and sudden lack of fear are doing that!

"Yes!" Mystic said. "I *can* do this!"

He had thought his sudden epiphany and growing confidence would send Trembly back wherever he had come from, but the red cat didn't move an inch. He sat on the path, solid and imposing, staring at Mystic with a horrible, knowing look. Mystic didn't know what to make of it. He was about to open his mouth and repeat his mantra (I *can* do this!), when Trembly began to smile.

It was a small thing at first, but it grew wider and wider until it seemed almost to float off the sides of his face. All his teeth were there, sharp and glistening in the low light. Mystic had never seen such a horrible smile in his life.

And then Trembly's eyes began to change. They darkened to black, as though someone had poured ink into them. They too began to grow wider and wider until they were twice the size they had been, and then three times. The red cat laughed.

Mystic was almost hypnotized by the horror before him. Trembly's eyes were dark, hollow tunnels in his face, and within them Mystic glimpsed a realm of nightmares and overwhelming horrors.

He knew that, if he stayed where he was much longer, he would become lost in those bottomless pits. There would be no escaping. Mustering all his survival instincts, he turned and bolted into the woods, only this time he didn't run blindly. He stayed on the same path he had taken out, knowing that Lili and Lulu would be waiting for him at its end. He didn't dare glance behind him to see if Trembly was following. He didn't know what he would do if he looked back and saw that solid mass of red fur and flesh barreling through the woods after him with horrors leaking from its hollow eyes.

What a mess! What a mess! Mystic thought as he ran. He had done everything Freedom had told him to do. He had breathed deeply, even managed to get back his confidence and positive thinking, but it hadn't helped a thing! It hadn't given him any power over Trembly at all. *And now he's even more terrifying and determined to destroy me!*

He was getting angry with Freedom. Everything she told him only filled him with false hope and led him into danger. *She's the reason I'm even in this situation.* But that thought led to another, one so terrifying it stopped him in his tracks.

What if Freedom is the one who is trying to hurt me? And then on the heels of that, came another. *And what if Trembly is trying to scare me back to sanity?*

From the distance came the crashing of something moving through the underbrush behind him. He turned to face it. He was afraid—almost deathly afraid—but his desire to understand the truth was stronger than his fear.

2

Trembly stepped into the clearing where Mystic was waiting. He looked like himself again; his eyes were back to normal—one gray, one green—and his mouth was the right size. He wasn't smiling but looked content all the same.

"How do I know which one of you to trust?" Mystic asked as Trembly sat, his tail flicking from side to side. "I feel like just a tool for you and Freedom to use against each other, and that neither of you actually cares about me."

"Of course I care about you, Mystic," Trembly said with his deep voice.

"How can I know that? All you do is terrify me."

Trembly chuckled. "I don't do that for my own amusement, Mystic. I do it to try and shock you back to reality before it's too late."

"Why couldn't you use kindness instead of fear? I might have believed you sooner if you had."

"It's not my way. It would mean lying to you the same way that Freedom is lying to you."

Mystic felt a sudden flare of anger within him. He almost opened his mouth to yell at Trembly but was surprised into momentary silence. He had almost started to defend Freedom and what she had told him; the words were right on the tip of his tongue.

But why would I want to defend her if I doubt what she told me? It didn't make any sense. But he thought back over his encounters with Freedom and relived the incredible feelings he had when he was with her. He had never felt even a fraction as good around Trembly. Mystic regretted stopping to talk to him again.

Why did I start having such violent doubts? Freedom hasn't given me any reason to doubt her, and yet I have. I think I've made a mistake. Maybe if I'd just kept running, I'd be with her right now.

"I told you the world is a dangerous place, Mystic," Trembly said. "You've seen some of that danger firsthand. Your goal in this life isn't to look for pleasure but to train yourself for all the dangerous and nasty things coming your way."

Mystic watched Trembly's eyes, certain they would once again change to black gaping holes, but they didn't. There was something hypnotic about them nonetheless, and he listened entranced despite his unwillingness.

"Look at the way the wild cats took advantage of your ignorance and weakness and got you to give up your home for Tiny. Now you're lost in your mind and confused. And on top of all of that you're homeless, too."

No matter how much Mystic didn't want to admit it, Trembly was right. He hadn't been prepared to face the nastiness in the world, and the other cats *had* taken advantage of him. It was true, too, that the world could sometimes be a bad place. It was entirely possible to look at what had happened the way Trembly said. It made everything more unclear, like trying to see objects in a room beyond a dirty window.

"Life isn't about playing around and looking for some paradise of pleasure and wellbeing," Trembly said. "It's about fighting, and you have to prepare for it. You're going to encounter all kinds of dangers, and you have to know how

140

to fight against them when they come."

What Trembly was saying was horrible and bleak, but Mystic could see how it might be the truth.

"I know it's hard coming back to the real world. But if you want to survive it, you need to see reality as it truly is, not how you want it to be." Trembly surveyed Mystic with his cold gaze.

"But I don't just want to survive, I want to live! I want to be as happy as I was before Bumpa left me!"

"But happiness never lasts," Trembly said. "And if you focus only on that and live for it, you'll wind up more depressed and hurt than you were before."

"So I should just be miserable all the time?"

"Of course not. You might be happy, sometimes." Trembly paused for a second as if savoring what he was about to say. Mystic wanted him to stop talking. He didn't. "But those moments of happiness are scarce, Mystic. You must accept it now. Life is simply not a happy thing."

Mystic wished he didn't know any of this, that he had never set out on this journey of self-discovery. *I may not have been really happy before, not like Freedom is, but I was a hundred times happier than I am now.*

Lost in his thoughts once more, he didn't see Trembly approach him. He jumped when he felt the red cat's touch on his shoulder; it was cold like ice.

"Let me show you the real world, Mystic." His voice was deep and resonant. "Follow me down the path, and I'll show you everything."

Disheartened, Mystic stood without comment and shuffled after Trembly like a lifeless zombie, following him

141

down the path. Before long, he started to recognize it, though it didn't look as bright and vibrant as it had when he had set out for the woods.

Everything looks so dull.

They passed Lili and Lulu's enclosure, but they were nowhere to be seen. A pang of regret hit him. *If I hadn't gone off into the woods, I could be in there with them right now getting ready for bed.*

"You see how nasty the world can be?" Trembly said. "The time that you need them to be outside to greet you and make you feel better is the time that they're selfishly inside getting ready for sleep, without a thought for you or your wellbeing."

Mystic watched the enclosure closely, hoping that Lili or Lulu would appear and prove Trembly wrong, but they didn't. That made him feel even lower than he had before.

They continued walking until they came to another familiar cage. It was the small, sad cage where Mystic had encountered the monkey earlier that day. It was incredible to him that it had been today. In his mind it seemed a week had gone by. There had been so many emotions and ups and downs. They had left him feeling exhausted.

"I don't want to go in there," he said. "I've already met the monkey, and he doesn't like me."

Trembly turned to Mystic with a secretive smile. "His name is Xoxo, and he and I are old friends. I'm sure he won't mind if we stop in for a visit." He stepped between the bars, and Mystic followed.

Xoxo appeared from beneath the same bush as he had that morning, although this time, Mystic noted with some satisfaction, he didn't leap out and try to crush him.

"I thought I told you not to come around and tease me," Xoxo said gruffly, but his voice lacked the power it had had earlier.

"I brought him here," Trembly said, flicking his tail contentedly.

"Well, that's fine then," Xoxo mumbled, "I guess. But why did you bother?"

"Mystic has been fooled and taken advantage of by some cats he thought were his friends," Trembly said. "Now he's deeply lost and confused. I thought you could tell him your story and prove to him I'm trying to help him. That I'm a true friend."

"No, that's okay," Mystic said quickly. "I understand if it's too personal for you to tell." He was feeling more depressed than he could ever remember, even more so than he had right after Bumpa had left. He didn't want to hear Xoxo's story. Just based on the monkey's appearance, Mystic knew it would be too sad, and he couldn't handle that right now.

"Actually, kid, I'd like to tell it," Xoxo said his voice morose. "It makes me feel better to talk about it, even though it hurts. It gives me a purpose, makes me feel worthy. It makes me feel like I still matter."

Mystic still didn't want to hear the story, but he couldn't hurt Xoxo's feelings. He felt that the monkey must not open up very often and was almost honored that Xoxo would open up to him, so he just nodded for him to start.

And a few moments later, Xoxo did.

3

Mystic was lost in the darkness. Some part of him was vaguely aware that he was dreaming, but it didn't make what he was seeing any easier to handle. Before his eyes were flashes of images so horrific he couldn't bear to look at them for more than a few seconds: Xoxo strapped to a table with wires running from his head, flickering lights and the smell of electricity, humans moving around him in long white coats. Those and many more. When Mystic pushed one away, another would take its place. The part of him that knew he was asleep also knew these things weren't fabricated by his mind but rather bits and pieces of Xoxo's story resurfacing.

Finally, they sank below him as he moved upward through the darkness, moving faster and faster, leaving the horrors far below, until he opened his eyes and took in the dull light of Lili and Lulu's bedding area.

Lili had been licking Mystic's back and stopped. She and Lulu towered over him, their faces bent close to his.

"You're not dead!" Lulu nearly shouted, and Lili thumped her head into his neck.

"Hush, Lulu," she said.

"I'm just glad he's not dead!" Lulu said, and Lili thumped him again.

Mystic tried to stand and found his body was stiff and sore.

"Easy, Mystic," Lili said. "You took quite a fall. When I woke up a little while ago, you were curled up on my thigh and I didn't know it. When I stood, you fell. I can't believe it didn't wake you."

Why am I here? Mystic wondered. The last thing he remembered was Xoxo telling his story, a terrible and horrific story, and now he was here. He had no recollection of coming here and curling up on Lili.

He felt empty inside, totally devoid of all emotion, satisfaction, or purpose. He couldn't even tell if he was alive.

He made it to his feet and staggered out into the bright sunlight of the giraffes' enclosure, but even the sun didn't fill the void within.

Lili and Lulu followed him out slowly, exchanging looks of concern.

"Your eyes are empty, Mystic," Lili said softly. "What happened to you?"

Another series of images flashed before Mystic's eyes. He blinked hard a few times to get rid of them. "They told me the truth," he said in barely a whisper.

"*Who* told you the truth? And what did they tell you?" Lulu asked.

"Trembly and Xoxo," Mystic said. "They told me the truth. They told me..." But he was not really sure what he was going to say, and after a moment he lost his train of thought entirely. The little bit of energy he had used to stand and stagger out into the day was gone. His legs shook, and he sat down hard on the ground. He wished he hadn't even woken up.

Lili and Lulu exchanged another look, and Lulu nodded. Lili lowered her head to the ground and made three low rumbling grunts. Mystic watched, not knowing why she was doing this and not caring at all. All he wanted right now was to sleep again. He dragged himself up once more, trudged back inside to where he had woken up on Lili's pile of hay, and curled up as tightly as he could. The warmth of his belly against his head was the only thing that made him feel anything. It was comforting. He wanted to stay curled up like this forever and never have to interact with anyone ever again.

-4-

Mystic couldn't fall asleep but didn't want to speak to anyone just yet, so he feigned sleep. At some point, Lili and Lulu came in, neither one speaking, and settled down in Lulu's hay pile.

A little while later, when Lili and Lulu's breathing had evened out and Mystic couldn't tell if they were asleep or not, the soft padding of feet approached them. At first, he was worried it might be Trembly returning, but as they got closer, he decided the footsteps were too soft. He dared look through squinted eyes.

"Hello everyone," Freedom said in her usual pleasant way.

"I'm sorry to have to call you, Freedom," Lili said in a loud whisper. "It's Mystic again. Something dreadful must have happened to him last night because he's not himself at all."

"Wasn't he with you last night?"

"He wanted to spend the night in the woods to prove he had conquered his fear," Lili said.

"We tried to convince him not to, but he was

146

determined," Lulu added.

Freedom just shook her head.

"And then this morning, he just seemed so...disconnected," Lili said, "as if there were nothing left inside him at all."

"You did the right thing calling me Lili. Mystic is in a state of shock, and he needs help. I just hope I can give it to him."

The giraffes exchanged a look of concern.

"We'll give you your privacy," Lili said, and she and Lulu clopped out into the bright morning.

What if she can't help me? Mystic thought. *If she can't do it, then no one can. I'll be like this forever.*

Freedom slowly approached him. He shut his eyes tight.

He felt the gentle touch of her paw down the length of his back, followed instantly by a flood of warmth throughout his entire body. It was as if she were instilling life in him again. Tears seeped from beneath his closed eyelids and made their way down his cheeks.

"It's okay, Mystic," Freedom whispered in a soothing voice. "Everything is going to be okay." She continued to caress his back while Mystic cried silently. Eventually, her paw slowed and then stopped, but she left it on his back.

"Please don't let me go," Mystic said softly, remembering what Trembly had told him, about how happiness never lasted. He dreaded the moment when her paw would finally fall away, leaving him by himself again.

"Why can't it last?" he whined.

Freedom replied without asking him what he meant. "Happiness coming from without never does."

"Why is it Trembly who's right and not you?" he said lifting his head and staring into Freedom's green eyes. He wanted to see her reaction, to see if she would squirm or try to hide her face, embarrassed, but she stayed composed as always.

"Trembly is right only if you believe him, Mystic, just as I am right only if you believe me. It's not an either-or thing."

"It's not about believing," Mystic said sadly and buried his face in his paws. "It's about what I see and feel. It's about what's *real*." He let out a strangled sob. When he had himself under control again, he continued. "And what I see is that happy times are infrequent and short-lived at that. And pain—all kinds of pain—is there no matter where I look. It never goes away but those few times it does, it comes back stronger than it was when it left."

"What you say is true," Freedom said, letting her paw drop from Mystic's back.

Her words were a punch in the gut, and Mystic felt himself falling backward as though off a tall cliff. He couldn't believe she was actually telling him that Trembly was right. He had hoped she would reject his notion as ridiculous and tell him something comforting as she had every time up to now. And on top of that she had removed her paw from him at the same time.

"Then why did you try to make me believe otherwise?" he asked, raising his head, tears streaming from his eyes. Freedom was still wearing her normal, patient smile, and that annoyed him. "Do you enjoy fooling me? Does it make you happy to lie to me?"

"I couldn't enjoy fooling you, Mystic because I never

have," she replied.

"But you lied to me, didn't you?"

"No, Mystic, everything I've told you is true. You're just confusing what I mean by happiness. You think happiness is *only* caused by what happens to you. But you forget the happiness that is the result of what you decide to think inside your head, Mystic. And happiness—real happiness, lasting happiness—only comes from within."

Mystic was still exhausted and confused, but what she said had caught his interest. It was the first time since he'd woken up that anything had. It felt good. Like something that was missing in him before had suddenly reappeared.

"It's so hard not to let fear swallow me up and take all my hope," he said. "And every time it does, I feel dead inside, empty. This time was the worst, though."

"I know it's hard, Mystic. And I know it's not what you want to hear, but you need to be prepared for it to happen again. Because the more you try to change, the more you practice being happy and positive, the more your fear will fight these changes"

"But why?" Mystic complained.

Freedom's tail flicked lazily back and forth. "Because you've been *taught* that it's natural to be afraid of change and the unknown," she said. "It's been so strongly wired into you, that your fears are trying to hold on to what they know. They're trying to survive. You need to keep practicing to change the way you see things. And then, slowly, your fear will become less intense, and you will start to consider the changes exciting and stimulating…but that takes work."

But Mystic wasn't focused on what she was saying

anymore; an image of Xoxo had popped up in his mind, followed by one of a human wearing a long white coat. "What about Xoxo, then?" he asked, suddenly sure he had poked a hole in her theory. "His tragedy was real! I don't remember everything he told me, but the things I do are horrible. You can't tell me he can just erase it all by thinking positively. You can't just think that you're going to be happy and then *be* happy. It's not that easy."

Mystic sat back, satisfied. He had finally stumped Freedom. She couldn't say that Xoxo just needed to find ways to be happy, because Mystic had taken that option away from her. He didn't think there was any other way she could justify her theory.

But as usual, Freedom stayed calm.

"Isn't it funny how we all prefer to fight to justify what hurts rather than fight to justify what could give us pleasure?" she said. "Xoxo has suffered like no other I have ever met, and while the horrible things were happening to him, it would have been nearly impossible for him to feel any kind of wellbeing."

"So then I'm right! Not everyone can be happy all the time—and you acknowledge it!"

"You're right, Mystic, not everyone can be happy all the time. What happened to Xoxo was an abomination…but it's over now. And as wrong and as painful as those things were, they've left him with more than just scars; they've also left him with a choice. It's not an easy one, but it *is* there. He can keep those awful memories alive, and keep reliving the pain endlessly like he is now…or he can let them go and move forward. He can find ways to look at his life in a more positive light. And if he does, hope and joy will return to him."

"You just don't want to admit that your theory doesn't always work," Mystic said. "Don't you think that sometimes the suffering can be so intense it can push someone beyond their ability to find happiness again?"

"It's true, sometimes the pain inflicted is so intense that happiness can never come back as greatly as it might have, or it could take many years for it to happen. But nothing is written in stone." Freedom smiled. "Like with Xoxo, it's still a choice. If they don't think they can ever be happy again, then they won't be."

"I guess," Mystic said.

"It's true. Just look at yourself as an example. You didn't suffer as Xoxo did, but happiness eludes you. You say it's not possible, and defend your belief that it's all some sort of scam, because it's easier to stay unhappy than it is to change." She must have seen the look on his face, because she held up her paw and shook her head. "I mean no offense, Mystic, we all do this at first. I did, too. We tend to believe only what we see around us to be true, that it's the only option, that it couldn't be anything else. But when we do this we give up all our hopes and with them our power."

Mystic was greatly annoyed that Freedom was making a lot of sense. Each time life had challenged him and caused him to feel terrible, he had taken this lack of success as an excuse to give up trying, to abandon his power. And he never took responsibility for it. Instead, he blamed Freedom's theory, or Trembly...even Lili and Lulu for his feelings. It was so much easier to play the victim than to take

151

responsibility for his state of mind.

"It's only me," he sighed. "*I'm* responsible for my own state of wellbeing and happiness, not anyone or anything else."

Freedom nodded. "Yes, Mystic."

He hated hearing it and knowing it was the truth. It was so much easier to think that his happiness was out of his hands.

"I miss the time before I knew any of this," he whined, "when all I'd do was have fun with Sarah and Bumpa. I had no questions or doubts in my mind. It was just perfect."

"Was it really perfect?" Freedom's eyebrow lifted slightly. "Because when Bumpa disappeared, you were devastated, and your entire life collapsed."

"That's why I have to find him!" Mystic said.

"And why do you want to find him?"

"Because it feels good to be with Bumpa."

"So the real reason is the need to feel good then, isn't it?" Freedom said. "It's about this incredible feeling you had when you were with him?"

"I guess so, yes," Mystic said, annoyed. "I know you told me to try to feel the way that I did when I was with Bumpa without him being with me, but that's just stupid! If everyone walked around happy for no reason every day, then no one would need anyone. Everyone would be alone. That's not life."

"You're completely right, it wouldn't be life if that's how it was, but thankfully that's not how it works," Freedom said. Her eyes glimmered. "If no one had to rely on anyone else for their happiness, everyone would be free. Doesn't that sound wonderful?"

"But I don't want to be alone. I love playing with Bumpa and Sarah and even Ulysses."

"I didn't say that being happy meant being alone, Mystic. Everyone would be free *together*, don't you see? If you're truly happy on your own, you stop being a prisoner to the needs of others. So when you're with your friends it's only for the pure pleasure of it and nothing else. And this…this is delightful."

Mystic thought about what Freedom was saying. The more she talked the more he saw she was right. He liked the idea of being with Sarah and Bumpa and experiencing just the pleasure of it in the moment. If listening to Freedom and learning what she had to teach could help him arrive at this place, he wanted to try.

But as he began to calm down and feel his hope returning, refilling the void inside him, a sudden vision of Xoxo seized all his senses.

A NEW START

Mystic saw the action unfolding behind his eyes. The vision bathed him with excitement and enthusiasm, making his heart pound joyfully in his chest.

He was helping Xoxo to escape his cage. The door was standing wide open, and Mystic was holding onto Xoxo's arm, pulling him toward the opening. A shadow of a person in a long white coat floated somewhere behind them, chasing them, but Mystic deftly outran it and pulled Xoxo to safety like a hero.

When the vision faded, he was left with a deep feeling of serenity. Freedom was watching him with her knowing smile.

"You said intuition could communicate with you through images in your head, right?" he asked her suddenly, not wanting to bring up that annoying pipsqueak but unable to help it. He had a feeling that what he had just experienced was a part of it.

"Yes, it can."

"And how do you know it's intuition?"

"Because it feels amazing and it feels right," Freedom said.

Mystic frowned. "But why didn't it ever come to me as

155

a vision? Before now it has only showed up as a voice and scared me half to death?"

Freedom laughed. "That's not entirely true, Mystic. When you came up with the idea to take Tiny to your home, that was your intuition trying to communicate with you. But you didn't always see it or pay attention to it, so it had to get your attention in other ways."

This was a surprise to Mystic. He had thought that only the voice was his intuition, but if he understood what Freedom was telling him, his intuition was really there all the time. He just didn't know how to see it, yet.

"What if you had a vision and it made you feel enthused...Would you follow it?"

"How do you think I ended up here?" she laughed again.

Mystic smiled at the thought of Freedom having visions about him.

"Just remember to carefully assess how you're feeling at each moment," she added. "Because your intuition is always speaking to you."

Hearing Freedom endorse his decision to follow his intuition made Mystic ecstatic. He couldn't believe it. Only a few hours ago, all he had wanted was to go back to sleep and die. Now he was excited at the idea of going to help Xoxo.

-2-

Mystic explained his vision to Freedom (skipping over the part where he had acted like a hero; he didn't want her to think he was full of himself), to get her opinion on it. He was

156

eager to get going, but at the same time hesitant to trust so fully in something that, until recently, had annoyed him greatly.

Freedom had been enthusiastic about his vision, but she told him something he didn't quite understand.

"Don't confuse physical and mental freedom, Mystic," she warned. Even though he hadn't fully understood what she meant, he had agreed not to. He was too excited to tackle this new project.

But once again, his stomach put his plans on hold by growling and churning. He had barely asked himself where he could find food, when the voice popped up and startled him again. This time, he succeeded in not becoming frustrated.

"Penguins," it said and then was gone as though it hadn't been there at all.

Penguins? What does that mean? I can't eat a penguin.

For once Mystic was hoping the voice would speak up again, but it didn't. Rather than let it annoy him, he decided to ask Freedom for her opinion.

"Do you know how penguins could help me get food?"

She turned to him, her eyes dancing with mischievous light, almost drooling as she spoke. "They have the most delicious fish you can find in the entire park. Why do you ask?"

"The voice, my intuition, it just came to me and said 'penguins,' but I had no idea what it meant."

"That's wonderful, Mystic! First a vision and now a perfect place to look for food! Well done!"

Mystic sensed the pride she was experiencing, and it

made him feel even better about himself. He felt like he was floating on a cloud—a cloud that was bringing him closer to Freedom.

His stomach growled again more insistently, pulling him out of his fantasy.

"Let's go get some food," she said and walked out into the giraffe's enclosure.

They waved goodbye to Lili and Lulu, who were happily grazing in the treetops, looking utterly content, and made their way across the park to the penguin habitat next to the old polar bear tank.

Freedom led Mystic down a set of concrete steps to a tunnel below. At the bottom, and down a short hallway to the right, was a large wooden door with a small hole cut into it. The closer they got to it, the more strongly Mystic could smell the fish lying just beyond. Freedom glided through the hole without a second thought. Mystic followed, but once on the other side he froze. The smells coming from the room beyond were delectable, but the room itself was dark and cold. Crates of fish stood all over the floor, some open, most closed. Two men were working on one at the far end, emptying fish into a silver bucket and then disappearing through a door at the rear.

Mystic crouched down to the ground, his ears flat against his skull. He hadn't been expecting people.

Freedom glanced at him, amused. "Are you okay?"

Mystic looked at her and took a deep breath. *You're fine. You're here with Freedom, and she doesn't look the least bit concerned. Nothing bad is going to happen.*

"Yes," he replied with what he hoped was more

assurance than he felt. He didn't want to talk about his fear; it would only give it more power. It would make it seem more important than it was. *Freedom is fine, and then so am I,* he decided.

The men made trips in and out of the room, sometimes by themselves, sometimes together. Each time they entered, Freedom ducked and dived into a safe place. Mystic followed.

"They're feeding the penguins," she whispered as Mystic watched the men with curiosity. "We just have to wait for the right moment."

Mystic marveled that she could treat all of this as a game. He made another decision: he wanted to learn how to do this, too, if he was going to enjoy everything in life the way Freedom did.

A few seconds later, it was the right moment. Both men had filled their buckets and exited the room together, leaving the crate unguarded. Freedom leapt from her hiding spot behind one of the crates and jumped toward the open one the men had been using. "Come on, Mystic, grab a fish!" she shouted joyfully, sinking her teeth into one and leaping back to the floor.

Mystic ran, grabbed one, and then leapt down behind her. They ran back toward the door with the hole.

As they got closer, Mystic wondered if he would fit through the hole—which his mind insisted had been a tight fit on the way in—with a fish in his mouth. This doubt triggered panic within him. He tried to calm down before it could grow and take over his body, but a sudden bang startled him. The men were coming back in through the door behind them. He was suddenly certain that he and Freedom would be caught. The panic, which had been only a small spark, erupted into a bonfire.

We'll never make it! His heart, which had been thumping with excitement, was now fluttering against his ribcage like a caged bird. *They've seen us, I know they have!* The panic was burning throughout his entire body now. He dropped the fish, bolted around Freedom, and through the hole in the door. Once on the other side, he didn't slow or turn around until he reached the top of the concrete stairs, out of breath and shaken.

Freedom was making her way up the stairs, leisurely and laughing around the fish in her teeth. Mystic began to feel very ashamed at the way he had just cut and run like that.

"I'm sorry," he said when she reached the top, and he hung his head, feeling incredibly stupid.

Freedom dropped her fish, licked her lips, and laughed again. "It's fine to run away when you sense danger. It's very sane to have that reflex. It could save your life someday."

"But what about everything we talked about before?"

"Getting frightened is all right, Mystic. The important thing is to not let this fear fester within you and stop you from trying again." Her voice sounded amused and she shrugged one shoulder, poking fun at him just the teensiest bit. "Maybe you could have checked if the danger was really real before you gave up?"

"Wasn't there any danger?" It seemed unbelievable that there hadn't been, yet it was somehow easier to believe it out here in the fresh air and the sunlight.

"No, not really." She smiled. "It was that fear of yours

getting in the way again. It stopped you from being resourceful, and made it so you couldn't think straight anymore…That's why you didn't come up with the idea of checking behind you to see if there was any real danger."

Mystic felt embarrassed.

"It's alright, Mystic. Fear is a good thing—like I said, it can save your life—but *only* if you stay in control of it. If you don't, then everything you'll do will end up being driven by it, and you can't live that way."

Mystic shook his head slowly. "I'm so stupid."

"Oh no! No, no, no, you're not stupid at all," Freedom said. "Just because you didn't succeed yet doesn't mean that you won't…unless you give up entirely. But I know you wouldn't do that. Just keep in mind that when you're learning, everything that happens to you is a step in the learning process." She looked at him warmly. "Please don't let a step trip you up and become a reason to feel badly about yourself, alright?"

Mystic knew she was right. It was his first attempt after all. Freedom had been there many times before, and she was more comfortable with it than he was. Besides, he wanted to impress her.

He nodded his head with resolve. "Okay. I'll try again for you."

"Why would you do it for me and not for yourself?" Freedom said. "I already have a fish, and my approval won't fill your belly. If you want to succeed in finding joy in doing things, you have to do it for yourself. Because if you only do them for others, the happiness you're seeking through their approval will always elude you. But if you do it for yourself, you'll be happy." She edged closer to him and nudged him gently with her shoulder. "And you know what else?"

Mystic shook his head.

"Those around you who really care for you will be happy simply because you are."

Mystic was surprised he hadn't picked up on this before. One of the reasons Freedom was amazing to be around was her confidence and happiness with herself. It always made him feel better about himself, too, which inspired him to attempt greater feats in his own life. The way she had said it just made so much sense to him.

"Thank you," he whispered, filled with love and awe.

"You're very welcome, Mystic. But now go get your food before they're done feeding the penguins. I'll wait here for you."

Despite the hiccup of fear in his chest, Mystic decided he would give it another shot, and he would do it for himself. The taste of the fish still on his lips and tongue was tantalizing, and his stomach was growling more and more persistently. He turned and stepped down the stairs to the tunnel below.

-3-

The closer Mystic got to the bottom of the stairs, the more his enthusiasm abated. The atmosphere didn't feel the same as it had when he and Freedom had come down together. The darkness, which he hadn't noticed at all before, now seemed everywhere. He wondered what could be hiding behind the shadows.

It just fits how I feel anyway, Mystic thought. *It's exactly as Freedom and all the wild cats have been telling him from the start. I need to change the way I feel about this and start to look at it positively.*

"Well, that's easier said than done," he grumbled.

"Do you really want to keep believing in and justifying your limitations?" Freedom called down the stairs after him.

"Oops." Mystic turned around to look back up at her. "You can hear me?"

Freedom was silhouetted against the sunlight behind her, but he couldn't see her face. She was sitting regally. He liked to imagine that she was smiling, but somehow down here in the dark it was nearly impossible.

The sooner I get started, the sooner it will be over, he thought, descending the last few steps. He began to notice sounds he hadn't before—mechanical hissing, squeaking, and from far-off a thumping. The landing at the bottom of the stairs seemed to be getting darker even as he looked at it.

He stepped down onto the concrete pad at the base of the stairs and turned right. Now he was facing the darkest part of his trip. The short hallway between him and the door with the hole in the bottom was darker than the nighttime when Mystic had traveled back and forth to visit Bumpa. He could see just fine, but there was something unsettling about it anyway. He was glad to know that Freedom was sitting somewhere behind him. If she hadn't been, he knew he would have found it very difficult to keep his courage up. He would have probably turned tail and bolted by now. Her presence was pushing him beyond his own limits of courageousness and helped prove to him that he could go farther.

Besides, if it was really dangerous, I don't think she would have sent me down here all alone. That thought helped to buoy his confidence.

He was only halfway across the dark hallway when something landed before him with a heavy thud. In the darkness Trembly's red fur looked almost phosphorescent, his eyes like they were lit from behind. Mystic felt his legs begin to shake with fear as all his previous encounters with the red cat suddenly returned to him.

"This is a dangerous place to be, Mystic," Trembly hissed like a venomous snake. "Do you know what will happen to you when those men behind the door capture you? They'll do horrible things to you, the things they did to Xoxo, like—"

Mystic felt his body and mind spiraling out of his control. He knew he had to stop it before he reached a point from which there was no return, where the shock overtook his system and shut him down.

Everything is okay, he thought abruptly, cutting off all other thoughts and erasing the horrible vivid images Trembly was trying to conjure up. *Everything is fine, it's perfect even. Trembly doesn't exist, he's just fear from some unknown place. He needs me to keep him around, and I don't want to anymore. He's an illusion. Nothing more than an illusion.*

"It actually feels good to think this way!" he shouted in Trembly's face.

The red cat looked taken aback for just a moment but then continued his poisonous hissing. "They'll catch you and

164

they'll destroy you. They'll use you for the most horrible and degrading experiments, like they did to Xoxo, and they'll make sure you suffer the entire time. Remember the scars on Xoxo's head?" Trembly dropped his bottom jaw and pulled his face into a twisted mask of agony.

Mystic tried to ignore him, but it was difficult. The horrible face was only part of it. Trembly's eyes were glowing in the darkness, two points of eerie green light floating side by side. Mystic felt his fear flare up again as once more those eyes pulled his attention fully, trying to drag him deeper into their depths.

Suddenly, something within him startled him into taking a deep gasping breath. He had not realized that he'd stopped breathing, but now with the sudden burst of oxygen, he could think a little more clearly. A mild sense of relief grew within him.

And then the voice spoke in his ears with urgency. "Look away, just look away, stop thinking about it, just do it, it's easy, just believe it's easy." It spoke quickly, running its words together so fast and so sharply that Mystic was amazed he'd been able to hear it.

This time the voice didn't bother him at all, and without even stopping to think whether or not he should listen to it, he squeezed his eyes closed tightly.

"Xoxo was one of the lucky ones," Trembly said. "There were others who weren't."

Mystic couldn't help but imagine Xoxo in his small cage, devastated, alone, and lifeless.

NO! NO, NO, NO! Mystic thought. *Don't talk about him!*

"Nothing bad is happening to you right now," the voice

said quietly and from far away. "Don't allow Trembly to control your imagination."

Yes! Mystic thought frantically. *Yes, I'm fine, I'm fine, I'm not hurt like Xoxo!*

"And you don't exist!" he finished aloud, roaring into Trembly's face once again. Trembly took a step back, surprised but retreating no farther.

It's a start, Mystic thought. Then he continued, speaking loudly and quickly to prevent Trembly from being able to interject. "I'm okay, do you hear me? You're trying to scare me with things that haven't happened yet. Why should I get scared now? Why should I sabotage myself from succeeding because of something that hasn't even happened and might not? Why not get excited that I might succeed instead? Maybe the men won't see me—have you thought about that?"

As Mystic was shouting, Trembly puffed out his fur so that he doubled and then tripled in size. His eyes darkened and grew as they had that night in the woods. Then he opened his mouth and bared his teeth, which were large and unruly. He began to hiss and yowl. The sound went straight through Mystic's body, piercing his mind like shards of glass. He fell to the ground, silenced, nightmarish images lurking just beyond his vision.

Trembly laughed a horrible, clotted laugh, worse than anything Mystic had heard so far.

I have to find a way to get out of this and fast! Mystic knew that he soon would be lost under Trembly's power. Last time Freedom had been there to rescue him, but this time, all on his own, he knew he had precious little time to act.

To find some way he could help himself, he dug deep into his memory and into the conversations he'd had with Freedom. Breathing deeply had helped a few times, and he tried that now, but it made him feel no better. The opposite, in fact. Then he recalled Freedom telling him he should listen to his intuition.

But how do I get my intuition back? It had retreated as soon as Trembly had started making that horrible sound in his throat.

I have to block it out. My intuition comes to me when I'm feeling better, and I need to find a way to do that now. That means not listening to the sounds Trembly's making. But how could he do that? Blocking them out seemed nearly impossible.

And then, like a patch of blue sky in the middle of a thunderhead, the voice came softly back to him. Mystic had been so lost in his mind figuring out a way to feel better that he had involuntarily ignored Trembly's hissing. Now Mystic felt slightly better.

"Freedom," the voice said.

Of course, it was obvious! He'd been so afraid he'd overlooked the most obvious thing that usually brought a smile to his face.

He summoned up an image of Freedom and focused on everything he liked about her: the way she moved, her smile, her voice, her energy. Without realizing it, Mystic found himself completely absorbed by these thoughts and the pleasant relief that came with them.

In his mind he saw Freedom—just a small cat compared

to Trembly—placing her paw on his lips and telling Trembly to be quiet, and he had. Then she had told him to leave, and he'd done that, too. The power hadn't been in her physical force but in her mind. She'd stayed calm and joyful, as she would have been with no danger around at all. It had robbed Trembly of his power.

Mystic realized that, as long as he tried to fight Trembly, the more Trembly would resist him and fight back. A twinkle of hope grew in his mind, and his intuition spoke again, a little stronger this time.

"Look at him without fear and have fun," it said. "Everything is just a game."

Mystic giggled at this thought, whether because it was a ludicrous thing for his intuition to say while he was trapped by Trembly, or because it was outright stupid, he didn't know.

Nonetheless, he assessed that he did have a choice. He could choose terror and stay cowed by Trembly's presence, or he could choose to have fun. After all, if he was going to die, why not die feeling happy? Whatever the outcome, why not choose fun?

He was feeling much better now. He was reenergized to find new ways to start feeling better and better still, and all of this had allowed him to steel himself for his confrontation with Trembly. More than that, he was almost looking forward to it. Where before there had been a sense of dread and terror was now only lightheartedness. He opened his eyes, prepared to confront the monster Trembly had once again become, but where Trembly had sat was now only an old, tired looking cat. His fur was lusterless and patchy, his eyes faded and weary. Mystic was shocked for a moment, thinking that Trembly had somehow escaped and another cat had taken his place, but it was really him. The sound was no longer coming from his throat, and the menace was gone from his eyes.

Mystic stood and walked a few feet to his left. Trembly didn't move. He stayed where he was, looking older than ever, staring at the place where Mystic had been seated.

Could I have really been scared by that cat? Mystic thought, amused. He was bathed by a feeling of elation. What Freedom had been telling him all along was true—it really worked! It was within Mystic's power, and only his power, to either allow his fear to grow or to shut it down entirely.

Before his thoughts could shift, he took a great leap, landed on the floor behind the deactivated red cat, and slipped through the hole in the door.

Once on the other side, Mystic immediately spotted the fish he had dropped only a short time ago. He approached it, feeling silly about how he had acted. There really had been no reason for him to be afraid. The men couldn't have seen him here. His fear had caused him to react rashly and stupidly. He hadn't even thought to turn his head and check before panicking. But instead of judging himself, Mystic remembered what Freedom had told him about this being just a step. He laughed as he grabbed the fish in his mouth.

Even the sounds he had heard as he came back down the stairs to retrieve his fish had been only the men moving the crates and opening and closing the door. Nothing more.

He walked back to the hole in the door, dropped his fish

through, and smiled—as he just hadn't thought of that before—and then went through after it.

Trembly was no longer sitting in the hallway, which now looked lighter than it had.

Mystic picked his fish up with a feeling of pride he hadn't known before. *I did it! I really, really did it!* He galloped up the stairs, eager to share his success with Freedom.

-4-

As Mystic made his way upstairs, he started to feel more and more energized by his happiness. He looked up to see Freedom, but she was no longer where she had been. He bounded up the stairs even faster but, once he reached the top, noticed that he was indeed alone.

He felt a wave of disappointment, which caused a cramp in his stomach. His intense joy had disappeared in an instant. He had already started to think of how unfair this entire situation was, when he realized what he was doing.

Once more, he was deciding to allow an outside event to hurt him instead of enjoying all the amazing energy he'd just experienced.

He also recalled Freedom had told him his happiness wouldn't come from her approval, but from his own.

It would have been nice to share my success with her, but she must have had a good reason for leaving, Mystic thought with just the tiniest bit of guilt. *Maybe there's another cat who needed her help more.*

He decided to stop complaining and celebrate with

himself instead.

I'm my own hero! he shouted in his mind. *I'm amazing and strong! I've annihilated Trembly's power over me, and I did it by myself!*

This kind of thinking felt odd to him at first—he wasn't used to thinking of reasons to sing his own praises—but as he continued, the elation he'd had coming up the stairs gradually returned. Before he realized it, he was feeling reinvigorated and was up on his hind legs, jumping around and shouting gleefully.

"I did it!" he shouted. "I defeated Trembly. I am powerful!"

Mystic was so busy jumping, celebrating, and shouting affirmations of his power, that he had missed seeing Freedom step out from the bushes nearby and sit down on the path. He only noticed her as he spun around. When he did, he dropped to all fours, his cheeks burning beneath his fur.

"You caught me," he said with a goofy smile.

"No, I actually helped you," Freedom laughed.

Mystic was about to ask her how, when he realized how for himself. "You weren't here because you wanted me to be happy for myself instead of relying on you to make me happy."

Freedom nodded.

"I only wish I didn't dance and carry on so foolishly in front of you," he said with a grimace.

"But I love the way you celebrate!" Freedom came to him and Mystic was even more embarrassed now. "No really, I love it!" she continued. "It was so contagious that I couldn't stay hidden in the bush any longer, I felt such a strong desire to celebrate with you!"

"What do you mean?" Mystic asked, feeling a little better after Freedom's kind words. "Didn't you plan to come out from your hiding place?"

"No, not really," Freedom said. "I wasn't going to come back. I only waited to make sure you made it out all right, but you surprised me twice! You successfully defeated your fear when you encountered Trembly by ignoring him entirely, and then you didn't let your disappointment steal your happiness when I wasn't here afterwards. It was incredible! You've achieved something really incredible today!"

Wow, Mystic thought. *Everything is just perfect. Even the things that seemed negative at first have worked out in truly amazing ways!*

"It seems every situation is an opportunity for something great," he said, "if you choose to look for ways to feel better and see things positively."

"Yes, absolutely," Freedom said. "And your willingness to change is admirable. You're going to perform miracles!"

"I do have one question, though," Mystic said, fearing that Freedom would soon leave. He was enjoying the conversation too much to let her go just yet, even if the fish smelled delicious and he had to eat.

"Go ahead, you can ask me anything, Mystic."

"When I was down in the tunnel with Trembly, my intuition came to me again and it told me something.

"Oh, yeah?" Freedom smiled as though she already knew what Mystic was about to say.

"Yeah. It said that everything in life was a game, and that's how you have to see it. Is that true?"

Freedom's eyes lit up at once, causing another shiver of pride within him.

"It's absolutely true, Mystic!" she said. "You see, your intuition is powerful, and you should listen to it. Everything in life *is* a game. It's just that sometimes we win, and sometimes we don't. But what matters is to keep playing, keep finding ways to justify our happiness!" She rubbed her head against the side of Mystic's neck, totally stunning him. Even his hunger and the delicious fish were forgotten momentarily as she nuzzled him and purred.

He began to purr, too, content in that moment and feeling a wave of great affection for her. *I love it! I love it!* he thought, his mind dancing.

A few minutes later, she stopped and looked at him seriously but with great tenderness. "You're remarkable, Mystic, you and everything you've accomplished today…you should be so proud of yourself. I think you're really beginning to see everything this path has to offer. And if you keep going down it, you'll be amazed by how your perception will change even more, and by what else you can achieve.

The idea of a greater feeling of joy than this was exhilarating.

"But for now, eat." Freedom smiled and then was gone, disappearing into the bush from which she had come.

Mystic was feeling wonderful. The fish had been delicious and well worth the trek down into the tunnel. He was licking the last of the oil from his whiskers when he thought about Bumpa. He couldn't wait to squeeze his trunk and tell him all about his adventure trying to find him. He wanted to tell him how much he loved and missed him. This thought energized him. He'd never told Bumpa exactly how he felt before, not as directly as he wished to now.

Mystic was enthusiastic about mastering his mind, his emotions, and how much more that would allow him to give to Bumpa. It wasn't only about what Bumpa could do for him anymore.

He was daydreaming about their reunion when he sensed the voice, his intuition, about to speak to him once again. This time Mystic made a conscious decision to welcome it happily and listen to what it had to say instead of becoming annoyed.

It was an amazing thing, he thought, changing his point of view. As soon as he accepted the voice instead of dreading it, its presence started to feel nice, very comforting, and reassuring. Mystic giggled at the sensation.

The voice, my intuition, it's only love. Its only reason for being is to help me succeed in being happier. The idea of it made him feel like he was surrounded by friends, like no matter what happened he would never be alone again. It brought tears to his eyes.

The voice didn't speak this time. Mystic sensed that it didn't have to. Now that he was more open to it, more attuned to its presence, it only had to give small nudges in the right direction instead of trying to drag him there. It sent up a picture of Xoxo, and Mystic latched onto it at once, his joy fleeting but intense.

I'm even more certain of what I want to do next! I want what gives me the most joy when I think about it! I'm going to help Xoxo!

Having a goal and a destination in mind made him feel good. Rather than wasting this good feeling by overanalyzing it, he decided to start off for Xoxo's cage at once.

The park was beginning to fill quickly, busy with children running and playing with great excitement. This time, Mystic didn't think about the possible dangers they posed. Instead, he paid close attention to his surroundings, and when a child got too close, he just darted behind a tree or a large rock, whichever was handy. It really was simple. When he had been controlled by his fear, it had seemed an insurmountable task, but now it was nothing more than a walk in the park.

This demonstration of his power gave him a great sense of freedom. He could choose whatever path he wished, and there was something liberating about that. By the time he reached Xoxo's cage, he was near to bursting with energy.

Three small children, a little younger than Sarah, were standing before the cage, watching with large, inquisitive eyes. Mystic thought about how he used to react in situations like this. Before, he would have lamented his poor timing in arriving just as three children were blocking his way forward. He would have relived his bad luck over and over until his day was ruined. He laughed at himself, remembering what Bumpa used to say when something like this happened.

Oh, Bumpa, you were always so patient with me. Trying to show me that everything was fine, that having to wait wasn't the end of the world, that we were free to do anything else we wanted to do. You spent so much time and energy trying to show me that there was no reason for me to complain as often as I did or to be so miserable. That I could stay happy instead and that it wasn't worth spoiling my joy because of something so trivial. You were so right, Bumpa.

He wished he could tell Bumpa how much he understood now, that he understood everything Bumpa had tried to do for him.

I will tell him, Mystic thought, trying intensely to instill within himself that trust that it would happen. Even if he had no reason to believe he would find Bumpa, he also had no reason to believe he wouldn't. Why should he imagine it not working out when he was free to imagine it working out in his favor?

The three children finally decided that the monkey was not of interest anymore and moved on, clearing the way for Mystic. They had run right past him without even seeing him.

Mystic crept out of his hiding spot and approached Xoxo's cage. He remained positive, but he wasn't without emotion. It was impossible to block out the memories of what had happened here with Trembly. He recalled the feelings of shock and lifelessness he had walked away from that encounter with.

When they'd met the first time, Xoxo had also told him not to come and tease him or any of the other caged animals. Still, Mystic was determined to go and see him.

XOXO

9

A NEW CHALLENGE

-1-

The delight Mystic had felt within him while thinking Xoxo's name couldn't be mistaken. Something important was waiting for him here.

If Trembly shows up again, there's nothing to worry about, he told himself. *I defeated him once; I can do it again. And there's nothing to fear from Xoxo either. He's in a cage and can't get out. There's no way they can hurt me. I am safe.*

The dangers he faced weren't only physical. They were in his mind, the way it could try to pull him down with all sorts of warnings and memories of unpleasant things that had happened here. But Mystic had learned better now than to imagine what could go wrong. He looked around and assessed that he was just fine; he was alone and everything was quiet.

As he approached, he heard a rustle of leaves. He couldn't see Xoxo but knew he was there.

"Are you hiding in your favorite bush again?" Mystic asked playfully, hoping to communicate to Xoxo he was coming as a friend.

"YES!" Xoxo shouted as he emerged from the bush on the opposite side from which he had jumped the last time. He landed before the bars where Mystic stood.

Mystic faked being startled, fell over backwards, and laughed. He really wanted to lure Xoxo into a friendly relationship (or at least a friendly conversation to start), and he was pleased to see a slight smile on the monkey's lips. He took it as a good sign.

"Isn't it funny?" Xoxo said. "Even though you knew I was going to do it, you were still scared because I came from the opposite side."

"Yes." Mystic beamed. "But this time I chose to laugh instead of getting annoyed, and it was great!"

"Yeah, well being free is a good remedy, isn't it?" Xoxo's smile disappeared, replaced by the sad expression Mystic had always seen.

"Yes, it is," he replied with a hint of embarrassment. "I'm lucky to be on the other side of the bars, but I'm sure we can find a way for you to be happy, even on the inside." His heart was bumping hard against his chest. He knew this was a dangerous gambit. It could either pique the monkey's interest, or it could switch on his anger and shut down the conversation right away.

"What arrogance!" Xoxo shouted, baring his teeth. "If you were inside and stuck like I am, you would never have dared say such a stupid thing!"

Xoxo's anger and lack of control reminded Mystic of the way he had been not so long ago. That helped him understand Xoxo's resistance. He knew the pain it could trigger, and he felt for him.

And it was easier for me. I was free; I didn't have bars to contend with. And I never underwent such suffering as he had. Mystic knew he had to act fast to get Xoxo back on his side before he lost him entirely, but he had no idea how to do it.

Without thinking, he started speaking, allowing his intuition to carry him. He was shocked to hear what came out of his mouth. "If you let me come in, I'll stay with you and help you get happy again".

Xoxo eyed him silently for a moment, and Mystic stood up to his gaze.

Am I nuts? What have I done? I don't want to go in there!

"You want to come in here with me?" Xoxo said, incredulous.

"Yes, I do," Mystic said, thinking, *Stop talking! Oh, stop talking!*

Xoxo smiled and showed his teeth but more pleasantly than before. "Fine," he said.

Mystic smiled but thought, *He agreed! Why did he agree? I'm toast!*

"You're an arrogant little thing, but I guess at least I'll have company for a while. And maybe you'll see what it's like to live in jail like I do. Maybe that will take some of the pep out of you."

Mystic felt trapped. He knew he had the choice to change his mind and walk away, but he would alienate Xoxo. There would be no hope of building a relationship after that. Now was not the time to lose his nerve. In fact, the entire time he was in front of Xoxo, he couldn't lose it at all. He must develop a more positive mental attitude.

Xoxo stepped aside, swinging his arm invitingly. "Well? What are you waiting for?"

What am *I waiting for?* Mystic wondered. *There's nothing terrible about having to be the monkey's friend for a little while, keeping him company and bolstering his spirits, right?*

"Remember, it's all a game," the voice within him whispered, and that made his decision. His anxiety was high, but he trusted what he was about to do.

"I'm ready for this game, then," Mystic said confidently. "Let's play jail."

"Well, whenever you're ready then," Xoxo said, a little confused, standing back from the bars, allowing Mystic plenty of room to come inside.

Before he could overthink what he was doing, or lose the small amount of confidence he'd built up, Mystic sprung between the bars. As he flew through them, his mind chattered on with doubt. *What are you doing? What if he attacks you once you're in there? Or what if Trembly shows up and they both attack you? What if his caretaker sees you and takes you away?* But it was too late for those considerations now. It was only fear trying to get the upper hand, and he refused to let it. If he could.

He landed inside the cage on a cold, black rock. Xoxo's cage was separated from the others, next to a large cement building, which blocked out the sun. That left the enclosure cold and dark. Instead of a warm bed of grass, the ground was dirt, and instead of luxurious trees, there were small stunted bushes.

And then there were the bars. Neither Lili and Lulu nor Bumpa's enclosures had bars on them. Mystic understood now why Xoxo felt like this was jail. The moment he looked out through them at the few passersby, he felt far from them, as if he couldn't be seen, heard, or reached. He felt isolated from the world he'd known so far. Despite being with Xoxo, he felt alone.

What in the world am I going to find in this place that will cause Xoxo to feel any joy at all, he wondered, a little frightened. He had been so certain before, and now he wondered why. What had made him think he could help Xoxo at all, especially in such dismal surroundings?

Xoxo leapt onto the rock beside Mystic and landed with a thud. He bent down until his face was only a few inches away. Mystic saw himself reflected in the monkey's large eyes and saw anxiety in his own big blue eyes.

"Well?" Xoxo asked with cynicism. "Are you happy now?"

A shiver ran up and down Mystic's spine. He tried to suppress it. He could not lose his nerve now.

-2-

Mystic's compassion for Xoxo had faded away, now replaced with horrible thoughts of what the monkey could do to him if he wanted to.

He could tear me limb from limb! Mystic felt trapped between Xoxo's intense gaze and the bars surrounding them. His paws began to sweat.

He closed his eyes and breathed deeply without making a conscious decision to do so. It was as though his body remembered the last time he had felt fear and was reverting to survival mode. When Trembly had tried to corner him in the penguin tunnel, Mystic had closed his eyes and tried to think of a way out of his predicament. And what had he discovered then?

That I need to trust and let go. Whatever will happen will happen, and there's no point in fighting against it. Nothing bad has happened yet, but if I continue to think negatively, it might. I have to let go. Let go. Just let it all go.

With that, he felt much better. It wasn't to say that all his misgivings were gone, but he trusted that everything would work out, and no matter how it did, he would enjoy it. Even if Xoxo tried to eat him whole, Mystic would go to his death smiling. Why should he taint his last moments with fear if he had a choice? The sensation of surrender produced a wonderful sense of calm within him, and he smiled.

"Are you meditating or what?" Xoxo asked.

Mystic was so relaxed that even Xoxo's sudden interruption didn't startle him. "No, I'm not meditating," Mystic said, surprised he wasn't scared to open his eyes.

Xoxo was looking at him, his expression brimming with confusion and questions. Mystic was pleased to see that Xoxo was no longer the terrifying monkey he had imagined. His big brown eyes were not the scary ones he had seen himself reflected in before. These were warm and round, with long, beautiful lashes. Even his nose looked softer than it had. His big teeth were certainly real, but they didn't look like gigantic killing machines anymore. They were only tools the monkey used to eat and nothing more.

Mystic smiled at Xoxo who, by some miracle, smiled back at him. It made him look goofy. He was actually cute, and it was incredible to think that he could have one mean bone in his body.

"So, have you discovered a way for us to be happy? Even in this gloomy place?" Xoxo asked. Mystic looked around. "Gloomy" certainly summed it up.

"I may have," Mystic said slowly, trying to work out his thoughts.

"Well, tell me!"

"For a moment I thought you wanted to kill me," Mystic said. "But you didn't."

"How is that supposed to make us happy? I mean…I can see how it would make *you* happy…"

"It's not just that," Mystic said. "It was something that came after, something I did because of that."

"What is it?"

"I had convinced myself that I was stuck in a horrible situation. At first, I was just terrified, and then…" Mystic paused, trying to think how to word what he felt so that Xoxo would understand it fully.

"And? And what?" Xoxo said with growing impatience.

"And I stopped resisting what was happening to me. I accepted it fully. Even if I had been convinced death was coming to me—and I was—I just surrendered myself to what was happening. I trusted that everything would work out how it would work out. And…"

Mystic was momentarily transported back to the night in the woods where he thought the trees had come alive and were trying to kill him. He'd blacked out, and when he'd awoken, he'd felt totally at peace with everything. Something in the act of surrender, the lack of resisting what was happening, had caused an intense state of joy within

185

him. Twice.

"And?" Xoxo said, even more loudly now.

"And I felt amazing!" Mystic shouted, staring straight into Xoxo's eyes. "I was so happy! I was facing death, and yet I was at peace because I wasn't fighting it!"

"Okay..." Xoxo scratched his head. "Well, what does that have to do with me?"

"Don't you see?"

"Uhhhhhh...not really..."

"It means we can do the same thing with your situation here!" Mystic shouted. "If we fully accept this prison as you call it, stop resisting what we can't change, just surrender to it, we might be happy here and now!"

Xoxo was just staring at him, and Mystic couldn't tell what he was thinking.

"Well?" Mystic asked, beaming. "What do you think about it?"

"You're out of your mind," Xoxo said wearily. "Do you really believe that, by accepting my worst nightmare, I can be set free from this place?"

"No," Mystic replied compassionately. "I'm sorry, Xoxo, I can't free you from here physically, but what I *can* do is find a way for you to experience more joy in being here now, and—"

"I DON'T WANT TO BE HAPPY HERE!" Xoxo shouted. "I want to be *out* of here!"

"I know, but—"

"No, you don't know! You couldn't even imagine, or you wouldn't have dared say such a stupid thing to me. You've disrespected me and you've hurt me."

"I didn't intend to," Mystic said. "I respect you greatly, and I'm being totally sincere when I say I believe I can help you. I'm not toying with you; I really want to help you, and I think I can."

Xoxo sighed, rolled his eyes, and headed back toward the bushes from which he always emerged.

Mystic followed him. "Please, Xoxo, give me a chance to at least try. Just one chance."

"I have no interest in your little mind games, and I don't want to get hurt again when you get my hopes up and fail. I'm finished with you."

Even though the monkey was no longer paying attention, Mystic continued to follow, trying to convince Xoxo he could help him change his life. He walked behind Xoxo and told him the story of everything that had happened since he had lost Bumpa. The only indication that the monkey was even listening was when he chuckled from the bushes when Mystic got to the part about being afraid of Xoxo eating him.

When Mystic stopped talking, he waited for a response. Eventually, one came.

"But what do any of your experiences have to do with me?" Xoxo shouted. "I'm not scared like you were. I've seen real fear, and it has no hold over me anymore. I'm stuck! I can't freely experience life like you do, and I can't meet amazing friends like you did! My life is an empty well of boredom and loneliness!"

"Well, you've met one new friend," Mystic said quietly. "Even if you did tell me not to come back and tease you."

"That still doesn't change the fact that I'm not free," Xoxo grumbled. "I'm trapped, and that can't be changed."

"Freedom told me that I shouldn't confuse physical and mental freedom." Mystic wasn't entirely sure what she had meant by that and hoped it might make sense to Xoxo, but apparently that wasn't the case.

"Well, that's just super!" Xoxo sneered. "That's going to help me get out of here so much faster!"

Mystic took a deep breath. He was trying to hold on to his good feelings, but it was becoming more and more difficult with Xoxo's negative attitude. "Look, Xoxo, you can believe me or not believe me. But just know that I'm going to stay here with you until I find a way to help you. I know there's a way."

"Do whatever you want," Xoxo said, but Mystic thought he heard a note of gratitude in his voice. "There's food and water inside if you want."

"Goodnight, Xoxo."

Xoxo mumbled something that could have been goodnight, and Mystic walked away from the monkey's hiding spot to give him some privacy. It would be best to let him alone for the moment.

After this interaction with Xoxo, Mystic couldn't stand still. Anxiety was growing within him. He paced along the bars, trying to release the tension in his body but knew it was his mind he had to calm. He needed to think positively.

I understand so much more now than I did a few days ago when I was as angry and confused as Xoxo. I mean, look at how much progress I've made. I'm sure I can figure out what Freedom meant by not confusing physical and mental freedom. And when I do, Xoxo will be fine, I know it.

His anxiety began to fade, and happiness grew within

him. Once again, he had not let melancholy get the better of him. He resolved instead to relax and trust that all would work out. It was remarkable how much easier it became the more he practiced it.

He wasn't really hungry yet, but the idea of a snack was tempting anyway. He went off in search of the food Xoxo had told him about.

-3-

Mystic found a small opening in a rock wall at the rear of the cage that was large enough for him to crawl through but which would have been ludicrously small for Xoxo. From within he smelled a mix of sweet hay, dust, and monkey.

He wondered again why Xoxo was in this cage instead of something larger and more accommodating to an animal his size, but he couldn't figure it out.

On the other side of the opening, he entered a small room. A pile of hay lay in the far corner. Closer to him sat a pail of water and some food scattered on the ground.

He approached the food and was hit by a sudden panic. It was a mix of dry leaves, roots, bark of all kinds, and not a bit of it was edible. It had never even entered his mind that he couldn't stay here if Xoxo's food wouldn't feed him, too. He lowered his head to the ground and sniffed to inspect the food more closely. Nothing looked the least bit appetizing. He pawed at it, hoping that maybe there would be something on the bottom buried beneath the top layer. Among the dry plants and old pellets, he noticed some dead insects.

"Oh gross," he muttered. "I hate dead insects." He sighed. He really had no choice. If he left Xoxo's cage, even if only to find food, the monkey would never take him seriously again. He would argue that Mystic could be happy because he still had the freedom to come and go as he pleased.

He hadn't been really hungry when he came in, but the prospect of food had awakened some hunger within him. Now he needed something to quiet his stomach. With a grimace, he bent over to crunch up all the bugs he could pick out of Xoxo's food, swallowing them with disgust and sticking his tongue out to get rid of the taste.

"Insects are very nutritious, aren't they?" the voice in his head said, and Mystic grimaced again.

"Yes, even dead." He was happy that he wasn't starved. The fish he'd caught earlier was still sitting comfortably in his belly. He finished his snack and then went to the bedding area.

The area inside the rock wall was the perfect size for Mystic. It felt safe and even cozy. The bedding smelled fresh, sweet, and looked very attractive. He decided to try it out. After his snack, he could do with some sleep. It had been a very long day. He burrowed into it, creating a tunnel, and it warmed up quickly with his body heat.

He was beginning to drift a little way toward sleep, when Xoxo's face floated up in his mind. Mystic felt bad for him. Here he was, comfortable in a warm bed, while Xoxo was asleep on the ground beneath a bush outside, probably shivering.

He would certainly sleep better in here than out there,

even if it's a tight fit.

He needed to at least try to get Xoxo to change his mind and sleep in here, too. That might be the first step in helping him to change his perception. Mystic crawled from the warmth of his comfortable nest.

"Xoxo?" he whispered loudly as he approached the monkey's secret spot. There was no response. He didn't want to stumble over him and frighten him, so he called again, a little louder this time. "Xoxo, it's Mystic. Can you hear me?" He waited a few seconds before he finally heard something from beneath the bush. It was almost inaudible, but it was a response.

"Why don't you come into the bedding area with me?" Mystic called.

"Because I'm not a dwarf like you!" Xoxo shouted suddenly.

"I know it's a tight fit, but once you're inside it's worth it! The bedding smells good and is warm. It's like not even being here, I promise! It will make you forget all about the bars!"

"No, it won't," Xoxo said sharply. "It will just remind me that I'm stuck here, that I'm not free. Who on earth would prefer being stuck in a small, cramped room instead of being out in the open with space and trees and leaves and fresh air?"

"Does sleeping under that bush make you feel free?" Mystic asked, curious. He'd never really thought about it before, but he supposed if he were in the same situation, he might feel like Xoxo. Especially given what Xoxo had been through.

"It doesn't make me feel free, but it's better than being stuck in that little cell."

"I'm sorry for bothering you, then. I thought I had an idea that would help," Mystic said, disappointed. He had thought it would work, or at least that Xoxo would have considered it. But the idea had come to him more out of guilt than joy.

Perhaps it isn't so surprising after all.

"It's okay, Mystic," Xoxo said tiredly. "I believe you thought you were helping, but right now all I want is sleep."

"Okay, I understand." Before leaving, Mystic turned back once more and said goodnight.

"Goodnight, Mystic," Xoxo said, and Mystic could swear he heard something in the monkey's voice that hadn't been there before. It wasn't happiness, nothing so grand as that, but he thought there was less sadness.

Mystic climbed back through the hole in the rock wall and padded over to the pile of hay. He was pleased that Xoxo had responded to his kindness in the way he knew how, but it wasn't enough. He knew how fickle the monkey's mood could be, and just because he was feeling less alone now didn't mean that feeling would last.

Why did I think I could do this? Mystic thought as he burrowed into the hay once more. *I should have started with something easier, something that would have taken less work, to help build my confidence. I feel like I did when I rushed into the woods that night and Trembly showed up. I had felt so confident and in control around Freedom, and then when I was alone—pfft! It was gone.*

He thought about that and about how difficult it would

be to combat Xoxo being negative each time Mystic suggested something.

And then from the other side of the room he heard a low hissing.

Trembly, he thought at once. A chill rocketed up his spine until he recalled their last encounter together. Trembly had been left old, sad, and defeated. There had been nothing to fear from him at all.

It's like Freedom told me. Fear is okay as long as it doesn't control me.

Mystic stood, arched his back, and hissed right back. "I'm not scared of you anymore!" he shouted with defiance.

Trembly looked normal again. He wasn't old and sick, but neither was he puffed up and imposing. He looked as he had when Mystic had first met him.

"Maybe you're not scared of me, but you're still scared," Trembly replied in a sickly-sweet voice. "And it doesn't matter if you're afraid of me, or afraid of yourself, it all comes down to the same thing in the end, and it's all good for me." He laughed and peered at Mystic with gleaming eyes. "It's delicious," he hissed.

"Why would I be scared of myself?" Mystic said, but his tone was less than convincing, even to his own ears.

"Because you were just thinking about how you'd never be able to help that poor, poor monkey out there," Trembly said with a cruel smile.

"No, I...I—" Mystic started, but then what would be the use of denying it? Trembly knew the truth, just as Freedom always did.

"Of course you were!" Trembly said with rapture. "And

it's such a wise way for you to be thinking."

"I wasn't doubting," Mystic said through clenched teeth, but his confidence was waning.

Trembly glanced at Mystic sideways. "Oh no?"

"No, I wasn't doubting that I could do it, I was just thinking it would be hard work and take some time." It wasn't entirely truthful, but Trembly's smug look of satisfaction was grating on his nerves.

"Well you can lie to me and you can lie to yourself, that's okay," Trembly said. "And you can try to convince yourself as much as you want that you'll be able to do it, but deep down we both know the truth. You were full of doubt, and that monkey is doomed. You'll never be able to help him. He's too damaged, and he won't ever listen to you. How could he? You're free. And even if by some miracle he did listen, you don't even know what you're doing. You'd probably screw him up worse than he is already. You're not Freedom, and you never will be."

"STOP!" Mystic shouted. "I can't and I *won't* let you pull me down! I don't believe you! I won't!" He dropped into the hay and put his paws over his ears. He wouldn't listen to another word from this nasty creature.

But that didn't stop him. Trembly laughed his horrible laugh and then spoke from within Mystic's mind. The feeling was vile, as if Trembly's words were grease sliding over the folds of his brain. Mystic felt each and every negative emotion attached to them.

"You're weak," Trembly whispered, his voice dangerously silken. "You won't succeed, it's an impossible task, and you aren't strong enough to handle it. You don't have the knowledge, the know-how that others like Freedom do. You're a nobody, an insignificant little nobody."

Mystic was crushed by Trembly's words. He knew they were just his fear trying to overtake him, that they were only as real as he allowed them to be, but he was losing his strength to battle against them. His body and mind conceded defeat to each and every word until he couldn't help but accept them as truth.

"I told you!" Trembly took a deep breath and shuddered with pleasure. "It feels wonderful to be alive within you, to get breath and life from your fear and doubt!"

Mystic knew the only way to combat him was to ignore him, to refocus his energy on something positive, but all his energy was being held in thrall by Trembly. He was barely able to lift his head and look at Trembly standing in front of him.

"A little depressed, are we?" Trembly chuckled. "Well, it's fine to be depressed, Mystic. As they say, the truth hurts, and I'm just being truthful with you here. It would be crazy if you *weren't* depressed."

Mystic tried not to listen and instead focus on why he felt the way he did, but it was difficult. *Why can't I do it anymore? I was able to do it before. In the tunnel outside the penguin enclosure, I was much more afraid than I am now, and I was still able to stand up to him. Why can't I do it now when I so strongly want to?*

"Wanting and doing aren't the same thing, are they?" Trembly said. "There are those who want, like you, and they will always want, want, want more and more. And then...then there are those who *do*, who act and take control.

But that's not you, Mystic. There's nothing wrong with being who you really are deep down inside." He bellowed with laughter.

Mystic hated Trembly. All the degrading things he was saying, all the pain he was inflicting, it was almost too much to bear. And yet, Mystic wondered why he had no trouble believing all those degrading things. Why did he accept them as truth simply because Trembly was saying them? He knew better than that. He'd proven he was better than that at least once, so why was it so difficult now?

He knew that, if he was going to get through the night and not be a gibbering lunatic in the morning, he would have to change his focus—and fast. He needed to court a new emotion that would lead to a better feeling, one that had nothing at all to do with Trembly or the horrible things he was saying. It was the only way he would be able to escape from this.

Mystic pushed his head into the hay and thought.

-4-

The hay was still warm and smelled just as sweet as it had when he first crawled into it. Mystic breathed deeply as he attempted to tune out Trembly.

I need to find a way to feel good. I need to find a way! He repeated this over and over like a mantra, all while smelling the hay. At some point, unbeknownst to him, he began to knead it between his pads as he breathed. The sensation conjured up a pleasant memory of a summer not long ago when he and Sarah had played together in a hayfield not far from the house. It was a wonderful day, and the hay had smelled as sweet as this. Perhaps sweeter.

I love it, he thought. *I love the smell and the feel—I love it!* It was as if he were reliving that afternoon with Sarah. He found he was beginning to feel better. He was even breathing more easily.

And like that, Trembly's grip on his mind and body released like a cramp letting go. A sense of calm filled the empty space it left behind. Mystic was filled with the knowledge that everything was all right again. His confidence returned.

Before this sense of wellbeing could dissipate, he intuitively raised his head and faced Trembly.

"I don't know or care what you've been saying," he said. It was as though someone else was speaking through him, someone powerful. He didn't worry about what would come out of his mouth but just let it come, certain each word was a finely honed knife thrown directly at Trembly's power. "You're right, I can't do anything for Xoxo. And do you know why? Because only Xoxo can truly help himself. All I can do is keep feeling good, show him it's possible to feel better, let go of the need to change him, and see what happens."

Mystic paused to savor the moment and the elation he was feeling. He couldn't see how Trembly was taking this, and he didn't really care. That was just a small and insignificant detail. The only thing that mattered were the words erupting from him like a divine message.

"Whatever Xoxo chooses to do and believe has no impact on my happiness. It's not my purpose to try to change him. It's his. I can only offer help if he decides he needs it."

The words flowed fluidly and were amazing. Mystic shouted with joy in his mind. *This is great! I love being responsible only for myself and my own happiness in this life!*

And the words kept flowing. "If I reach my goal and remain happy no matter the situation, it will inspire Xoxo to at least try and maybe even succeed. And then he'll be able to tap into his happiness with ease!"

"It won't be as easy as all that." Trembly's voice was not as powerful as it had been, but it was still strong enough. "I may not be able to reach you directly as easily as I once did, but I can still haunt Xoxo so much that he will never find happiness. He will be blind to yours and will only see false attitudes and manipulation. I'll make sure of that. He'll never believe he can do what you do. He'll be depressed and lonely forever."

Trembly's words were disquieting. It was incredible the lengths he would go to in order to maintain his grip over Mystic, and now over Xoxo. Mystic would have to remain on his guard and continue to practice his refocusing power. He had experienced firsthand how fear could easily crush all sensations of hope and enthusiasm. He wanted to build up his resolve against it, like Freedom had. Trembly would be watching and trying to ferret out weakness in him always.

But those thoughts were leading him down a path on which he could sense hopelessness. He cut them off immediately. He had nothing to prove to anyone—not Freedom, not Trembly, not even himself—he just wanted to feel good.

Trembly was still staring at him as if expecting another rebuttal, but Mystic received another intuitive flash. Rather than give Trembly the squabble he wanted, Mystic decided to listen to what his intuition told him.

He moved deeper into the pile of hay until he found a comfortable spot, curled up, and closed his eyes. The only thing he wanted to think of now was the coziness that enveloped him and the sweet memories that flooded over him with each inhaled breath.

Very quickly, Mystic felt at peace and started to fall asleep. He didn't think of Trembly's presence or of how he would help Xoxo achieve his happiness. He only breathed deeply, relishing the smells and sense of comfort he had found in that moment. And before long, he was asleep.

-*5*-

When Mystic awoke, it was morning. A dull shaft of light filtered in through the hole at the front of the bedding area, but he didn't open his eyes yet. He was floating on a wonderful feeling of freedom. Part of that was his gratitude to his intuition, which had arrived and helped him so greatly last night.

When he opened his eyes to the dull room he checked to see if Trembly was still there, but as he had guessed, the red cat had vanished once again.

He stood and stretched, excited at the prospect of the new day before him. It was pristine like the ground after a fresh snow. He set no goals to mar this day, either, except for the one of feeling good for himself.

And that will be challenging enough! he thought happily.

Mystic hopped down off the hay pile and made his way to the food scattered on the floor to see if anything new had been put out during the night. It was the same picked over food from yesterday. Finding nothing to his liking, and not yet being quite desperate enough to eat pellets, he went outside.

The first thing he saw was Xoxo and Trembly talking in the far corner of the cage. His belly tightened for a moment before he reminded himself that there was nothing to be worried about yet. Nothing had happened, and Xoxo might not even listen to Trembly's poison words.

Trembly gave Mystic a defiant smile and turned back to whisper something else to Xoxo. That done, he made his exit, leaping through the bars of the cage and into the thick underbrush beyond.

Mystic ignored him and wandered over to Xoxo, who was sitting with his arms crossed across his chest, looking sadder than he had before.

"Good morning, Xoxo," he said. "Thank you for letting me use your bed. It was one of the best night's sleeps I've had since I left home."

Xoxo said nothing but shrugged.

"I also had the most disgusting meal of my entire life!" Mystic laughed, remembering the taste of the dried out bug husks on his tongue. "Dead bugs are pretty gross."

"If you knew you had to eat that every day for the rest of your life, you wouldn't be laughing about it," Xoxo said.

"Yes, you're right…Maybe we could try hunting some live ones today?"

"There aren't any bugs around here," Xoxo said with disinterest.

Xoxo was free to react as he wished and Mystic did not want to impose any of his thoughts or beliefs on him. If he wanted to be negative, it was his choice. Mystic shrugged. "Okay."

"*Okay?*" Xoxo said, his voice sharper than before. "What do you mean by okay?"

"Just okay. What more do you want me to say?"

"Say that it's terrible!" Xoxo shouted. "Say that it's sad and that you pity me!"

"I won't do that, because it doesn't feel good," Mystic explained. "Just the same way that trying to force-feed you my beliefs doesn't feel good. I choose to let you be the way it makes sense for you to be."

Xoxo shook his head. "I was right about you yesterday. You're nuts!"

Mystic grinned. "Actually, I am and I love it."

Xoxo eyed him for a moment as if unsure what was wrong with him. "How can you go around being happy like that?" he snorted finally.

Mystic couldn't believe it. Already his decision to stop trying to convince Xoxo what he should do was paying off. It was touching something within the monkey.

This gave him an idea. "Freedom told me something a while ago that might help you," he said. "She told me that in order to be happy, you need to find all the reasons you can to trigger a feeling of wellbeing within you. And before you know it, it will happen naturally. Soon, it will be a habit. Just keep practicing." Mystic was aware this would have driven him nuts only a few days ago, but he didn't worry now about how Xoxo would react. In fact, he decided to share his feelings with the monkey to let him know it was normal to feel that way. "At first her advice made me angry, but after a while I listened to her…I did what she suggested, and it worked! Thanks to her advice, I just do, say, think, and focus on the things that make me feel good."

"But you can't *always* do what you want!" Xoxo shouted. "Do you think I'd stay locked up here in this prison if I could choose to do what makes me feel good?"

"Of course not."

"See?" Xoxo said. "If you were in my place, you wouldn't be happy."

"Xoxo, I *am* in your place, and I'm happy."

"It's not the same!" Xoxo shouted. "You've only just arrived, and you can leave whenever you want! I can't ever leave this place, so you can't tell me it's the same!"

"You believe and think what you want, Xoxo," Mystic said kindly. "There's nothing I can believe or think for you."

"But I thought you were going to help me," Xoxo said.

"I can't help you change the limits you've put up in your own mind. I can only be happy for myself and break down my own limitations. You can follow me on this journey and maybe come away from it with the tools to do this for yourself, but I won't follow you down your path of negativity."

Mystic was surprised by his words. He sounded like Freedom and realized that, once again, his intuition was speaking. But instead of the raw, protective power it had used with Trembly, it was now reasonable and calm.

"I can inspire you to greater things," Mystic explained. "That's how I can help."

"So if you need to seek happiness, you're going to leave me then," Xoxo said. "No one can be happy in this place."

"No, I'm not leaving you," Mystic said. "There is a way to be happy here, and we can find it together. You just need to believe that it's possible."

Xoxo looked uncertain but slightly hopeful, which Mystic gave him great credit for. It was as if whatever Trembly had been filling his mind with was starting to dissipate, as though Mystic's peaceful state of calm was more powerful than Trembly's despicable agenda. It reminded him of the power he had witnessed when Freedom had placed a single paw on Trembly's mouth. Mystic wondered if he was starting to realize this same power when a wave of shame submerged his mind.

How can I imagine being anything like Freedom! He shrugged. *She is so perfect, beautiful, smart, agile...*

But Mystic couldn't think like that. It hurt and gave Trembly the power to attack again. He had to keep feeling good, and this was not the way to do it!

10

THE POWER OF SURRENDER

Mystic knew that, if he wanted to be happy, he shouldn't be harsh with himself. After all, even if he wasn't as powerful as Freedom yet, he had banished Trembly yesterday, and Xoxo seemed to want to listen to him rather than Trembly this morning.

Why wouldn't I allow myself to think I'm realizing the same power Freedom has?

He felt enthusiastic and jumped when he noticed Xoxo looking at him, bewildered.

"Ok!" Mystic calmed down. "Let's go and see if they've put out new food."

"I hate eating," Xoxo said.

"Really? Why?"

"Because I hate going down there," Xoxo said, gesturing toward the rocky area where Mystic had spent the night.

"Okay," Mystic said, "but you don't hate eating then, do you? Just the place."

"I guess so."

"Then wait here a second." Mystic held up a paw. "I've got an idea."

He ran to the rock wall and disappeared into the hole. New food was scattered across the floor. It had a pungent odor.

"Uck," he said with a smile. "Monkey food."

For a moment, his brilliant idea faltered. He wanted to bring the food out to Xoxo, to show him that, just because it was given to him in this place, it didn't mean he had to eat it here, too, but in Mystic's mind it had all been so simple. Now, standing here, staring at the food without hands to pick it up and carry it, he thought it would be much more difficult than he had anticipated.

As soon as he had that thought, his belly tightened—as if this word "difficult" had done it.

Is that really possible? Could one word do so much damage so quickly? Mystic had used this word many times in the past when everything had already seemed difficult to him, and he'd never experienced this reaction before. Now, though, with his mood so elevated, it seemed to carry more weight.

Mystic smiled. His attitude was so different now, that now even negative words had become taboo. His understanding of the wisdom Freedom had imparted was so much greater than it had been. He felt like shouting out in joy.

I'm so lucky...so blessed that I have a great friend like Freedom! And all of this thanks to Bumpa's departure!

That froze Mystic's thoughts instantly. How could Bumpa's leaving him be a blessing? The idea that something as devastating as losing his best friend in the entire world could be anything but tragic was shocking.

He shook his head. *No, no, it's not possible.* At once he decided to push that idea away and concentrate on the project at hand. He had to think of a way to transport the food outside without labeling the process with that crushing word, "difficult." He tried to find another way to express it and was amused by the ideas that popped into his head. Finally, he landed on one that seemed right.

"I'm sure there's a way, I just need to find it," he giggled as it felt much better.

This new discovery was as exhilarating as all the others had been, and he found himself excited about being more conscious of his words in the future.

Once he stopped thinking of the situation as difficult, an image popped into his mind. It showed Xoxo's hands with his agile fingers. "Of course!" Mystic said, jumping. "It's so obvious!" He was amazed he hadn't seen it sooner, but didn't let that discourage him. He'd succeeded!

He swept the seeds, plants, roots, and insects into a pile before him and surveyed it. It would do just fine.

Mystic ran back outside to Xoxo, who hadn't moved a muscle.

"Come with me," he said, panting.

"Where?" Xoxo asked, immediately distrustful.

"Inside the feeding area. Come and help carry the food."

Xoxo gazed at the rocks then back at Mystic but didn't move.

"Look, what do you really want from life?" Mystic asked.

"I want to be free, you know that."

"Why do you want to be free?"

Xoxo rolled his eyes. "Well, that's obvious, isn't it?"

"Tell me, anyway." Mystic giggled a little. He remembered becoming angry with Freedom when she had teased him in this same way.

"Because I want to be able to do anything I want!" Xoxo shouted. "I want to run and jump and meet friends, to eat under the sky and not in that concrete cell!"

"And why do you want all those things?"

"Why are you asking me all these stupid questions?" Xoxo said. "Do you think I need a reason for wanting all those things?"

"No, you don't need a reason, and you don't need to justify to *me* why you're doing something. But if you want to do something, it's because it *gives* you something, doesn't it?"

"No, it doesn't give me anything. I do things because I want to do them, that's it. Because it feels good!"

Mystic smiled at Xoxo satisfied.

"What is it now?"

Mystic leaned in. "You do it because it gives you pleasure," he whispered triumphantly. "And you know what? It's the best reason to do something! No other reason in the world is better than this one!"

"I guess so..." Xoxo said, but Mystic could tell he still wasn't entirely convinced.

"Well, if everything you want to do is because it gives you pleasure, then that's the only thing that you're missing here, locked up in your cage. So, why don't you decide just to be happy? To feel good right now for no reason other than that you can?"

Xoxo stared but didn't say anything. He looked like he was understanding Mystic's words, which made Mystic want to jump with joy, but instead he finished his point.

"Why should you decide to wait—to delay your happiness—when the choice is up to you? You can't change your surroundings, and if you wait for them to change on their own, you might never be happy. But your mind, the way you perceive your surroundings, is changeable—and right now!"

Mystic didn't want to argue or try to convince Xoxo—he'd given him the information, it was up to him to decide what to do with it—and so to avoid this, he started back for the feeding area.

"Come on!" Mystic called over his shoulder.

Xoxo started to yell out, detailing the reasons he was wrong and the reasons it wouldn't work, but Mystic ignored this. He wasn't going to kill himself trying to convince Xoxo.

Then, as Mystic climbed through the hole in the wall, he heard footsteps rushing up behind him.

"I'm not coming because I believe you!" Xoxo called as he ran. "I just don't want that other cat, Trembly, to come back while I'm all alone."

Mystic wasn't fooled by Xoxo's show of bravado (he could hear that Xoxo was interested in the things he had said), so he disappeared through the hole into the feeding area. Xoxo came through a moment later, squeezing himself through the narrow opening more easily than Mystic would have guessed.

Mystic padded over to the pile of food and nodded to it. "Take a handful," he said.

"What, that's it?"

"Yes, that's it," Mystic said. "You have hands with agile fingers, and I don't, so if we're going to eat outside in a more

209

pleasant atmosphere, you'll have to carry it for us." He smiled as Xoxo dipped his hands into the pile and easily clutched a huge handful. He crawled out through the hole and then made two more trips before all the food was outside.

"There!" Mystic said, leaping onto the ground and pawing at the pile of food, searching for anything edible. "You can eat your food outside instead of in that cell!"

Xoxo looked around dumbstruck. "Wow," he whispered.

"Wow is right," Mystic said, still pawing through the food. "I think these are the same dead bugs I ate yesterday."

"It was so simple," Xoxo said in awe. "I was so focused on being here, being trapped, I couldn't see that I could make this one thing better for myself."

"We all do that sometimes." Mystic was hoping that the monkey wouldn't get down on himself for missing what now seemed so obvious.

"And if I can change *this*, maybe there are other things I can change, too. Maybe..." Xoxo hesitated for a moment, as if scared of saying what was on his mind. "Maybe I can have a happier life…even in here."

Mystic nodded eagerly.

"Thank you," Xoxo whispered, looking around at his surroundings as though for the first time.

"You're welcome," Mystic said.

-2-

Xoxo was eating and chewing his food with apparent delight, looking around, as if still in disbelief that he was

210

actually eating outside. Mystic watched him with great pleasure.

On the other hand, he felt no enthusiasm at all looking at the dried bugs Xoxo picked out and set aside for him. His stomach was growling loudly, he needed to eat. But he wanted something good, not dried up old bugs. He wanted the wet food Jean or Pete sometimes bought for him. It was juicy, smooth on the tongue with the wonderful smell and taste of fish.

Mystic began to drool. His stomach lurched and churned.

This is torture! Why am I focusing on what I don't have, like Xoxo was? But my stomach hurts! How can I ignore that? He could feel his stability starting to slip, which he didn't want Xoxo to see.

Xoxo pointed to the bugs. "I've saved these for you," he said in between munches.

"Ah!" Mystic said, feigning surprise. "That's so nice of you!" He approached the pile with a grimace of disgust, which he tried to hide and gulped the bugs down with no pleasure, not even tasting them. But even after the rather sizable pile was gone, his stomach was still complaining. He needed to eat something more, but what?

"It wasn't enough, was it?" Xoxo said as if reading Mystic's mind.

Mystic grinned. "And it was disgusting."

Xoxo burst out laughing. "It looks like you're getting the whole experience of being me now."

The monkey's laughter surprised Mystic. It was the first time he'd heard him laugh, and it transformed Xoxo into a gentler sounding animal. He didn't even feel upset that Xoxo was laughing at him. Instead, he felt like sharing in his good mood.

"I'm glad I could make you laugh," Mystic said.

"I couldn't help it—you have a bug wing caught in your front teeth."

Mystic rubbed his teeth against the fur of his front leg and noticed he was feeling better now than he had before. Somehow, switching his attention to Xoxo's laugh and good mood had removed the pain from his stomach. *Even pain can be decreased simply by not focusing on it anymore,* he thought with wonder.

He explained to Xoxo that he was feeling better and why.

"Really?" Xoxo said. "Do you really believe that what you think can change what your body does?"

Mystic remembered thinking about the canned wet food and drooling over it. "Yes, absolutely it can!" he said with renewed energy and enthusiasm. He'd gotten another idea, one he wanted to share.

"Close your eyes," he told Xoxo.

"What? Why?"

"We're going to try something," Mystic said, excited.

"Why aren't *you* the one who has to close his eyes?" Xoxo said, mistrust creeping slowly into his voice. Mystic could understand why the monkey might not like experiments and surprises, but this wasn't going to be bad at all.

"Because I've already tried it myself, but before I can come to a conclusion, I need to make sure it works for you, too."

"Is it going to hurt?" Xoxo asked in a small voice very

unlike his usual one.

"I would never hurt you," Mystic said softly.

"Don't you remember my story? I told you when you came here with Trembly."

"I remember only bits and pieces," Mystic said. "The day you told me—"

"You went into shock," Xoxo finished for him. "I thought maybe you had. You left here that day running and screaming as if your tail were on fire."

"I'm sorry I don't remember it, but I don't want to hear it again if that's all right."

"It's fine," Xoxo said. "Actually, I used to love talking about my horrible story. It made me feel somehow important, like I mattered more, but today I'm realizing that, every time I retell it, I relive it. It takes a little piece of me."

"So, you don't mind if we don't talk about it and if I don't know your full story?"

"Well, I *do* mind a little. But I'll try to accept it. I'd like to see what it changes."

"Thank you," Mystic whispered, relieved. "You're quite courageous, you know? And quite a fast learner, too. You've picked up this concept much quicker than I did. I admire you."

"Really?"

"Yes."

Xoxo looked astonished. "Wow! I used to tell my story to try to impress others, to feel important, but I've just impressed you by *not* telling it."

"Yes, you did!"

"Wow," Xoxo whispered again. "I used to think I was a

hero because I suffered—that I needed to suffer to matter."

"Yes, you did suffer, and no one can deny that," Mystic said. "But you're not a hero because you did. You're a hero because you're willing to overcome that suffering and to try to be happy in spite of it. This is an amazing step forward for you. I'm actually in awe of you."

Mystic couldn't believe what he had just said. It was his intuition speaking through him again. It caused joy within, and seeing Xoxo's shiny wet eyes staring at him, he knew the monkey was moved by it. It was another kind of power he held within himself. Not the power to influence or dominate, but to provide peace and kindness. It was simple, but it was amazing.

He wanted to hone and refine this power as he had his others. He knew the exact way. He must let go of his need to control it and trust it would work as he needed it to. And it seemed that, by helping Xoxo, he had enhanced his abilities to do this—as if by helping Xoxo, he was really helping himself.

-3-

"So," Mystic said, shaking off his thoughts, "shall we go forward with this test or not?"

Xoxo blew out a pent-up breath. "Okay," he said. "But is it really necessary for me to close my eyes?"

"No, I suppose not. But it would be better."

Xoxo seemed to consider for a moment before finally conceding. "But if you scare me, I'm opening them right away."

"That's a deal." Mystic asked Xoxo to move to a large flat rock that would be more comfortable than the ground and to close his eyes when he was ready.

Once Xoxo was relaxed, with his eyes closed, Mystic began.

"Imagine where you would like to be when you're free," he said.

"I don't...know what free really is," Xoxo admitted, embarrassed. "I was born in a cage with other macaques like me. We were all friends, and—"

"Okay, okay," Mystic said, hoping to stop Xoxo from reminiscing too deeply about his painful past. It would spoil the test if he became sad and depressed. "Where would you choose to be if you weren't here in this cage?"

"I would be with other macaques, like I was when I was younger," he replied. "It was the best time in my life. We were all happy together. That was before they took us and separated us. Before they—"

"Okay," Mystic said. Xoxo seemed unable to stop reminiscing about his worst times, and Mystic had to be vigilant. "Go back to your friends."

"It was so amazing," Xoxo said, his features smoothing out. "We loved to jump and joke and play tricks on each other. There was a lot of joy."

Mystic noticed a slight smile had appeared on Xoxo's lips. "Can you feel that emotion right now?"

"Yes! I actually can! I can't believe it!"

"I know." Mystic smiled. The first step had been a success. He knew that thinking about a past event would often bring up the feelings associated with that event. But

215

today he wanted to try something he hadn't considered before. Now he wanted to see if the same thing could be true of an event that hadn't happened. Something that was totally in the mind.

He chose his words carefully now. "You said that, when you get out of here, you would like to be back in a place like you were before, with other macaques like you, and be friends with them, right?"

"I would love it," Xoxo said a little wistfully.

"Can you imagine that? Can you visualize what it would be like?"

"I can try," Xoxo said, and Mystic was once again taken by the monkey's willingness.

"Okay, just picture it for a little while, imagine what it's like, and then when you feel comfortable, stop and tell me what happened."

"Okay, I'll try."

Mystic stayed silent, watching Xoxo to see if there was any change. Nothing happened for a moment until, suddenly, Xoxo's face broke into a sunny smile that grew wider and wider until it looked like he was about to cry.

"What's happening?" Mystic whispered, not wanting to break the silence but unable to help himself.

"It's so real," Xoxo whispered back. "The peace, the love, the joy...it's all so real." He breathed heavily, obviously moved by the emotions he was experiencing.

Xoxo had said the word Mystic had been wondering about. He had said it felt real. His hunch had been accurate, then.

Xoxo laughed. "I wish I could keep my eyes closed

forever. Can you believe that? Just after telling you I don't like having my eyes closed?"

"Does it feel more real than your life out here?" Mystic asked.

"No," Xoxo said after a moment's consideration. "It just feels real, as if it really exists, even though I know it's just in my mind."

"Then who's to say it isn't real? That what you're seeing now isn't what's truly happening and everything out here is a daydream?"

Xoxo opened his eyes. "That's it, you're talking crazy again, and now you've spoiled my wonderful dream. And here I am, back in the *real* world."

Mystic barely heard him. "How do we know what's really real?"

"I believe reality is what my emotions make me feel," a voice said from nearby. It startled both Mystic and Xoxo, who turned and saw Freedom standing just beyond the cage.

"Hi Freedom!" Mystic called, his voice still a little shaky from being startled. "Do you know my new friend, Xoxo?"

"I actually do," she said, smiling and nodding to Xoxo. She coiled backward and then sprung, her lithe body shooting though the bars like a small black arrow.

Mystic was speechless as he watched her. So much beauty, so much elegance. He could watch her jumping forever. He stared at her, hoping she wasn't reading his thoughts. She landed effortlessly on a rock a little way away.

"Are you in love?" Xoxo whispered loudly in Mystic's ears.

Mystic looked at Xoxo intensely but said nothing. His

cheeks were on fire beneath his fur.

"Don't worry, I won't say anything," Xoxo giggled.

Freedom gracefully stepped over to them.

"Hello, Xoxo," she said.

"Hello," he replied, looking confused. "I'm sorry, but I think you're mistaken. I don't think we know each other."

Freedom smiled. "Oh, we've never been introduced, no. But I know you. I know just about everyone in the park, though they don't always know me."

Mystic watched Xoxo's face closely, and the confusion he saw there made him smile. It was the same confusion he had felt when he'd met Freedom the first time, and the memories it called up were entertaining looking back on them now.

"So, do you really believe what you said about your feelings being the only reality?" Xoxo asked.

"Absolutely. I can perceive the same situation in an endless number of ways depending on how I'm feeling when I look at it. It's as if the outside events are almost influenced by that."

"But don't those outside events cause your emotions in the first place?" Xoxo said. "How can you influence them when they're already influencing you?"

As Mystic watched their conversation with great interest, his intuition came to him. It was strong this time, pushing him to open his mouth and see what came out.

"It's not just outside events that influence how you feel," he said, enjoying each word as he would a tasty treat. "What you think can also change how you feel. As a result, how you experience a situation will change, too. You just experienced the power your thinking can have on your emotions, didn't you?"

Xoxo shrugged. "Did I?"

"Yes!" Mystic exclaimed, no longer able to contain his excitement. "You imagined your life away from here, living with other macaques and having fun, which caused emotions and feelings. And it all felt real, didn't it?"

Xoxo nodded.

"So there's your answer. Emotions can be caused by things that are happening to you, outside events, but they can also be caused by what and how you think."

"Well, how does that help me?" Xoxo frowned.

"It means that whenever something happens to you that causes emotions you don't want to experience, you don't have to stay a victim to them. You can change them as simply as changing what you think about. It means you're free to feel any way you want to. You're free to transform any emotion from negative to less negative and, with some work, even positive."

"Yes!" Freedom cried from the side. "Congratulations, Mystic, that's it exactly!"

"Thanks," Mystic said shyly. He had almost forgotten that she was there, and her praise came as a surprise. He'd only been excited at his understanding, and in focusing only on that, he had impressed her! She was looking at him with tremendous pride. It made him feel wonderful.

"But wouldn't that mean you're in denial?" Xoxo said. "I admit, it did feel good to imagine being free of here, but the truth is I'm stuck here. Only now it feels worse because I've experienced what I'm missing."

Freedom turned to him. "We don't deny that you're stuck in this tiny cage, Xoxo, I don't think anybody would. But you are denying that there are ways to feel better, even in this situation. That there are ways for you to experience more pleasure day to day."

"Oh really? Well, I'd sure like to know what they are because Mystic hasn't found them yet."

"He's found some," Freedom said kindly. "They might not be the best ways for *you*, but I think he will keep working until he finds those. Right, Mystic?"

Mystic looked around the cramped little cage with a flutter of unease. The longer he looked at it, the less sure he was exactly *how* he would pull that off.

"Uh, sure," he said finally. "Of course I will." He felt no conviction and hoped that neither of them noticed, but Xoxo was smiling with vindication.

"I can do it," Mystic said with confidence he didn't quite feel. Xoxo's smile faltered a little, and Mystic calmed down. "The only thing that's troubling me is the lack of food here for me. I'm so hungry, and there's nothing to eat."

"Why don't you just go and get some?" Freedom asked. "You know where to find food in the park now, don't you?"

"Yes, but if I leave the cage, then I'm cheating."

"Who would say that going to get food is cheating?"

"Xoxo," Mystic whispered, glancing at the monkey who turned away, pretending to be interested in something in the dirt. But Mystic wasn't fooled and knew Xoxo was paying attention. "If I leave the cage, I'm not like him anymore. I'm free, and I'll lose credibility in his eyes."

"So you think that, in order to help someone who's

suffering, you need to suffer as much as they do?" Freedom said, amused.

"Well, I have to experience his life."

"You really think that bringing more suffering and pain into this situation will help anyone feel better?"

"But if I'm not in the same situation that he is, he won't listen to me or believe me," Mystic said. "When I come up with a way for him to be happier, he'll say it only works for me because I'm free. He won't even try it."

Freedom glanced at Xoxo, who was dragging his fingers back and forth in the dirt, making intricate patterns. "What Xoxo believes or doesn't isn't your responsibility, Mystic. You need to be inspiring, so inspiring that no one can resist the urge to want to be like you, even if you have what they think of as advantages over them."

"But can I still stay in the cage with Xoxo?"

"Of course, you can." She smiled. "You can do anything you want, anything in the world, as long as it gives you joy. And you don't need permission from me or anybody else. Just think about what is best for you and follow your intuition. Because, how can you expect to help others if you don't know how to bring joy to yourself?"

"You're right." Mystic wasn't one hundred percent sure—it still felt a little wrong to go and get food while Xoxo was stuck here—but his intuition said he should follow her advice.

"Go get some food and have fun then!" Freedom said.

Mystic approached Xoxo, who was still focused on the lines he was drawing in the dirt.

"I'm going to get something to eat," he said softly as he

221

approached. "But I will come back, and I will help you."

"Do you promise?" Xoxo asked, staring at Mystic with his warm brown eyes. Mystic couldn't help but feel a little sad at the look of melancholy on the monkey's face, as though a part of him doubted Mystic would return at all.

"I promise I will. And while I'm gone, I'll keep thinking of how to help you. I just really need to get something to eat, or I won't be able to help anyone."

"Well, I think I'll be going," Freedom said cheerfully. "I don't think you need me anymore right now."

Mystic wished he could ask her to stay, or even to share his meal, but he knew she wouldn't be leaving unless she needed to. She had come to help, and she'd accomplished her goal. Now she was off to provide help to someone else who needed it more.

The thought of a fish went a long way toward lifting his spirits. He could almost taste it on his tongue, greasy, oily, and delicious. He began to drool, which amused him. The fish was only a picture in his mind (albeit a very vivid picture), and his body was already beginning to respond as if it were right in front of him, ready to be devoured.

He really could call up any feeling just by controlling his thinking. This afternoon's revelation was a powerful one.

He leapt out between the bars and landed on the path that was deserted and calm. As Mystic set off toward the penguin enclosure, he thought about how he could help Xoxo feel freer while still trapped behind bars.

This time, getting the fish was a breeze. His mind tried to trick him and recall images of the men that had been there before (and, of course, Trembly). But he remembered what Freedom had told him and mastered his fear. He was so in control of it that he didn't even carry the fish out with him. He happily devoured it where he found it with great intensity and pleasure.

Climbing the concrete stairs, his full belly swinging beneath him, he reflected on how good it felt. He had been starving only a little while ago, and now he was completely sated.

I should never take food for granted, ever! he thought. *Even the dead bugs provided me enough energy to get here today, and as disgusting as they were, they were a gift.* It was true, but Mystic didn't believe he would ever feel the same satisfaction with a belly full of bugs that he felt right now.

The energy the fish had given him moved him to jump, twist, and even scratch his claws on the bark of a tree. It felt so good to feel full again. It was only after he was inside the cage, still bounding and dancing, that he saw Xoxo sitting very near where he had left him, looking sad.

"Thank you for letting me get the proper food," Mystic said, not wanting to bring up Xoxo's sadness yet. "I hadn't realized it, but I was starting to get depressed not having enough of the right food. Good food is an important ingredient for feeling alive and happy!"

"I guess so," Xoxo replied, not turning around.

Mystic could see that Xoxo was not doing well at all. He

wouldn't be able to joke him out of his sadness.

"What's wrong?" he asked kindly, going closer. "I wasn't gone for that long. What happened?"

"Trembly came."

"Oh?" Mystic wasn't really surprised by the news, not after Trembly's threat to do exactly that during their last confrontation. "What did he tell you?"

"He told me you wouldn't be able to help me…That you wouldn't know how because you don't understand what it's like to be here all the time. That you could leave whenever you want to and get whatever you want to eat."

"And did you believe him?" Mystic asked carefully. He didn't want to put the idea of belief into Xoxo's head if it wasn't already there, but he had to know exactly what he was dealing with.

"I tried not to. I didn't want to, but he was very persuasive. I tried to do what Freedom told me and think about how you don't need to suffer like me in order to help me but...it's just so hard. Trembly said you were too selfish to help me, that all you're concerned with is your own happiness."

"I *am* concerned with my own happiness, but your happiness is a part of that," Mystic said with a smile. "I wasn't happy because I was free, and I wasn't trying to get away from you. I was just hungry, that's all. I ate the right food for me, which has given me the energy I need to continue to help you. And look, I came back just as I promised I would."

"I guess so." Xoxo gave Mystic a sidelong glance. He looked like he wanted to believe, and that was a good sign.

"It's the truth."

"Well, I guess I can understand that," Xoxo said, turning a little farther. "I know that, when I'm hungry, I'm not very easy to be around and not much good to anyone."

"That's all it was," Mystic said, feeling the shift in Xoxo's mood. "And besides, in leaving to get a fish, I had an idea."

"Really?" Xoxo asked, turning all the way around. His morose expression had disappeared, replaced by a look of cautious optimism.

"Yes! I realized I hadn't given enough thought to the small sources of happiness that are all around us. Like the food. I'd never thought before that food could produce such an amazing sensation, but today I've seen it can. And I believe the same thing can be true in here. There is something—something we haven't been looking at in the right light—that will assist us in finding happiness."

"You're saying that there's something *here*, in this place, that can make me happy?" Xoxo said, looking around the cage.

"I don't know for certain," Mystic didn't want to lie to Xoxo and tell him there was for sure. His own perception of the cage was very negative, and the idea of finding anything here that could lift their mood seemed like a long shot, but all the same he felt it might be true. "We just have to believe there's something and that we can find it. What do you say?"

Xoxo looked around once more and then back at Mystic. "If you have the courage to at least try, then I want to try, too," he said.

"Perfect!" Mystic shouted and jumped in place a few

times, overtaken by the connection he felt with Xoxo. "Let's start!"

-5-

Both Mystic and Xoxo were silent, buried deeply in their thoughts. Xoxo was grappling with what Trembly had said, trying to push it far from his mind, while Mystic was trying to change his heavily negative thoughts about this place.

He couldn't help but hate it here. It was cold, dark, and faraway from all the life and energy of the park. It felt as though the world had moved on and left them behind. It caused a gulf of loneliness within him. It was hard not to be swallowed by it.

The food he had found had helped him, but the energy wouldn't last. He knew he had to think harder, act faster. If he didn't, the lonely feeling would devolve into negativity, and it would be even more difficult to struggle out from beneath that.

How can I do this? Mystic screamed at himself. *Everything about this place is depressing and ugly.*

"There's no obligation for you to look at it," the voice in his head replied.

"What?" Mystic was so lost in his thoughts that he'd almost missed the voice.

"What?" Xoxo asked from behind him, startling him.

"Nothing," Mystic said, suppressing a laugh. He didn't want to share anything about his intuition with Xoxo yet; there was enough to focus on now without confusing the issue.

226

"But you said something," Xoxo persisted.

"I must have been falling asleep and starting to dream."

"That's incredible that you could fall asleep like that. I wish I could do the same, just sleep—go off into my dreams and escape this place."

While Xoxo had been talking, one word stuck in Mystic's mind and echoed over and over. *Escape.*

"That's it!" he shouted, making Xoxo jump. "Nobody said we have to look at it!" The words his intuition had said suddenly became clear. "We don't have to look at it, or touch it, or interact with anything here if we don't want to. We can just close our eyes!"

Xoxo was looking at him like he was nuts again, but that didn't dissuade Mystic.

"Come on, let's close our eyes and see what happens," he said.

"I don't see the point, Mystic. It's the exact same thing you had me do before, and it left me more depressed afterwards."

"It's not the same thing," Mystic said. "This time you won't picture anything, you'll just shut your eyes and see what happens. That's all!"

"We won't see anything; our eyes will be closed."

"Please, Xoxo, don't be so childish."

"Fine, you do it and I'll watch you. If it works, maybe I'll try it. It seems pointless to me."

Mystic was upset that Xoxo was being so combative and wouldn't even try. His fear of failure started to grow when he remembered he couldn't force Xoxo to cooperate. He couldn't force him to see anything from his point of view. If

Mystic was going to do this, he had to do it only for himself, for his own happiness. It wasn't about success or failure but about the joy the process would give him.

That helped him to put his priorities in order. He took a deep breath and let it out.

"Okay," he said, his annoyance behind him now. "I can't force you to try it, and I can't force you to see it my way. I can only do it for myself and satisfy my own curiosity. Then we'll see what happens."

"Thank you," Xoxo whispered, looking truly grateful.

Mystic realized then that what Xoxo was saying and doing wasn't because he was against him in any way. He was just scared—scared to suffer even more than he was already suffering. Mystic found he had judged his new friend too quickly and too harshly. He decided to make an effort to be more indulgent in the future.

-6-

Mystic had no idea what to do next. So far, nothing had changed except that his mind had started to yammer loudly, dredging up all his doubts about his idea working.

There must be a solution. I just haven't been able to find it yet, but it's there. I know it's there. I have no doubts. When he thought that, the cacophony in his head stopped immediately, and the small voice of his intuition struggled out from under all the noise.

"Breathe, listen, and feel," it said. He knew what the voice meant by *breathe*, but he didn't know what he should be listening to or feeling. Those were just abstract ideas.

They didn't make any sense.

He screwed his face up as he thought, furrowing his forehead. Xoxo asked if he was okay.

"I am," Mystic said. "I just need to find some clarity here; it's still a little foggy."

"Would it help if I sang you a song?"

"What?"

"A song," Xoxo said. "You know, a bedtime song, something calming. One of the older macaques in the group I lived in used to sing it to us."

Mystic considered the proposal. *What could it hurt? It might even help me to let go of everything in my head that's unnecessary.*

"Okay," he said. "But if I ask you to stop, stop, okay?"

"Deal," Xoxo said, and a moment later he started to sing.

Xoxo's voice melted Mystic's heart with its softness and warmth. It was beyond anything he had ever heard in his entire life. Pete loved to sing. He would sing when he lay down in the sun or even doing the gardening. It seemed to relax him and brought a lot of joy to the family, but his voice was nothing compared to Xoxo's. There was a purity here, softness and love.

Mystic's body relaxed so deeply that he sank down to the ground. All the tension he had been feeling before was gone now. All he had left in his mind was love for that moment and that experience.

Then it hit him. He was *listening* and *feeling*, exactly as his intuition had told him to do. Having his eyes closed helped him focus even more thoroughly on the emotion in Xoxo's voice, and he could feel the music within himself, like a physical presence in his body. It was an entirely new way of focusing. It was incredible.

The only part of his intuition's message that he had fully understood at first had been *breathe*, and he focused on that now. He felt the air flowing in and out of his nostrils as soft as gossamer, flowing down his throat and then back out again with ease and without thought. It was incredible that he had never truly focused on his breathing before.

The song was coming to an end; Xoxo's voice was getting softer until it was gone entirely.

Mystic was totally relaxed and at peace. His mind was quiet, free from all the disturbances he'd felt moments ago. It didn't feel like moments, though, it felt like years.

In the space left behind after Xoxo stopped singing, Mystic noticed for the first time that it wasn't actually silent. Each sound he heard now was like Xoxo's song had been. They swarmed to him, drifted into his ears, each one simple, elegant, and pure. And when one was gone, another took its place, just as alive as the one before it, until they created a sensation that was soft and tingling.

It made him much more aware of his body, leaving him open to all kinds of new sensations. The soft breeze that ruffled his fur was electric and full of life. The ground beneath him was no longer bare dirt studded with rocks, but a strong, unbreakable surface that flowed into him like liquid energy at each place it touched his body.

A fleeting notion passed through his mind that this would be difficult to explain to Xoxo, and then just as quickly, it was gone.

What Mystic was feeling didn't allow him to escape

reality as he had thought but connected him with it more intensely. He heard birds he had never heard before, their calls a symphony of sound. He heard the wind gliding through the trees like sheets of silk, people talking in the distance like the babbling of a distant brook...There was so much more going on around him than he had ever thought possible. Once he had closed his eyes, had focused on his breath and on the sensations of his body, the shattering noise in his head stopped. And this silence in his head made his full immersion in this environment possible. All the beauty surrounding him could freely flood him with delightful sensations because nothing in his head prevented him from receiving it.

As he became more aware of the present, he could even hear his breathing. He had never heard the sounds of his own life before, the gentle rasping of his breath and the liquid thumping of his heart. It took him to a place of deep serenity he had never known existed before. He stayed there, motionless, focused on his breathing. It was too good to do anything else.

As he focused and listened to his breathing, he gradually traveled further within himself, as if being pulled on a small invisible thread. He had never thought it possible that such endless space could exist inside him, so alive and full of joy, encompassing all the possibilities in the world just waiting to be discovered. It was a sense of freedom that nothing could take away from him. This was his space, his world, and here he was more powerful than he had imagined.

The first sensation from the outside world Mystic became aware of was Xoxo's impatient pacing back and forth before him. He heard the monkey's eager grunts and even felt his longing gaze as Xoxo watched him intently.

"What's happening?" Xoxo said, his voice full of anticipation. "Please tell me what you're seeing!"

Mystic wasn't the least bit annoyed by Xoxo's interruption. He was experiencing a state of mind unlike anything else he'd ever known, where nothing could upset him and nothing mattered. Everything was love, joy, and happiness.

But even in this state of bliss, he couldn't keep Xoxo waiting forever.

"I'm not seeing anything," he said without opening his eyes. "I'm *feeling* it. Everything inside and outside me. There's no separation; everything is connected."

"Oh," Xoxo said, sounding confused. "I'll just wait until you're ready to explain, okay?"

But talking about his experience had doubled the intensity of Mystic's wellbeing. A bolt of love like none he had ever felt before struck him, radiating throughout his body in a millisecond. It was so intense and so real that tears dropped softly from his closed eyes, pattering against the parched dirt beneath him.

It became difficult to continue on like this with his eyes closed. He felt his awareness contracting back to its normal state, but he didn't worry. He trusted it could expand again if he repeated the experiment of silencing his mind.

Mystic took his time and surveyed his surroundings. Some great change had taken place. The cage was the same but no longer felt the same. It didn't have the same negative power over him as it used to. He looked beyond the bars and noticed all sorts of wonderful things he had never noticed before: the colors were more intense, the shapes had more depth, and the space between them contained life where he had never seen it. It was as though he had only been seeing in two dimensions up until now.

He had never been aware of such beauty. The birds flitted happily from tree to tree, the blue of the sky enhanced the white of the clouds floating majestically overhead...everything was in harmony with everything else, including this cage. Mystic felt no judgment for it anymore. It was there, it existed, that was all.

"I felt pure love," he said suddenly and dreamily. "It had no expectation and no judgment, it was just there. We block it with all the negative things in our head, but we don't destroy it. We *can't* destroy it. It's always there."

"How do you know that?" Xoxo asked.

"I can't say for sure, but I felt it. I know it's true."

"So how does that help me feel freer?"

"I don't know...I guess it's just good to know it, to be aware of it. Doesn't it make you feel better to know there's something out there that loves you unconditionally?"

"No," Xoxo said sharply. "If something was there, really loving me, then why am I here? And why would my mate Cocoon have died? Where is love in all of that?"

Mystic had no answer that he knew how to present to Xoxo without causing him more anger and sadness. It was tricky, but he decided to try anyway.

"I felt as though we don't understand the whole picture," he said. "We only see bits and pieces of it. If we want to make our lives better and learn to be happier, we must not lose our trust."

"Trust in what?" Xoxo asked angrily. "Trust that everything is *fine*? That everything is just *perfect*?"

But Mystic wasn't upset by Xoxo's reaction, nor was he deterred by it. Even to his own ears, what he was saying wasn't easy to hear or comprehend.

"Maybe we can't *always* trust," he whispered kindly. "But maybe we can try to do it as often as we are able to handle it. For instance, right here and now in this cage."

"You want me to trust that everything is fine here?" Xoxo said. "That I'm here for my own good and that there's a reason for me being here? That I should just blindly trust that everything will work out for the best?"

Mystic smiled at Xoxo and nodded. He could tell that Xoxo's anger was building, but he didn't fear the monkey now as he had yesterday. Xoxo stormed to the bars, grasping them in his hands.

"The only goal we can have is to embrace life and trust that everything is love," Mystic said. "Even if it's hard to perceive it as such, we have to try."

"And what would that change?" Xoxo asked, his anger replaced now by sadness.

"It makes everything lighter and easier to deal with. It creates hope and therefore more joy. It helps us move on past the tragic and harmful things that happen and let go of them faster."

Xoxo turned around, his brown eyes wet and rimmed with red. Fat tears were trundling down his cheeks. "Do you think Cocoon is loved, too?" he asked, his voice breaking.

"It's what I felt, Xoxo...I feel that we're all loved eternally and unconditionally. And it's what you can believe if you choose."

Xoxo burst out crying and grabbed Mystic in his arms the way Sarah would a teddy bear, sobbing hard. "Thank you," he whispered, his voice shaky and tired. Tears dropped into Mystic's shiny gray fur and stuck there like stars before disappearing.

Mystic hugged him back and let him release all the sadness that had been building for years.

-*8*-

Xoxo pulled back from Mystic's shoulder with a sniff and wiped his wet cheeks with the back of his hands.

"All that time, I was haunted by emptiness." He was looking at Mystic while he spoke, but Mystic thought Xoxo wasn't really seeing him. He was lost in his own thoughts. "The moment you said that Cocoon was loved, it was as if the space around me was suddenly overflowing with her presence. It was only her wellbeing and love; no negative thoughts came with her, none of the bad memories that used to come attached to it."

Mystic said nothing. He was puzzled by Xoxo's reaction to what he had said, but at the same time he was confident Xoxo would work it out and explain as best as he could.

"And I felt loved," Xoxo said, "loved for no reason at all,

but just...just loved." A long silence followed as he seemed to be working something out in his mind. Finally, he leaned over and whispered to Mystic. "She's happy," he said. "I felt it—she is really happy."

Mystic assessed Xoxo's face, which was now totally relaxed and free from all his sadness. He looked like he was in a state of shocked awe.

Something magical has just happened here. And I'm the one who initiated it. I did it! Mystic felt like jumping around, filled with a sudden joy, but didn't want to startle Xoxo's delicate peace. Instead, he celebrated in his mind. *I did it!* he whispered fiercely. *I have Freedom's power to help others, and it's the most incredible thing in the world. I have no idea how I did it, but I'm sure Freedom can tell me.* At the thought of Freedom, Mystic began to imagine the pride she would feel when he told her about his revelation. While he was picturing this, Xoxo stopped gazing emptily and looked around with real wonder in his eyes.

"Everything's different," he whispered. "Everything looks...just different."

"How?"

"It's more alive," Xoxo said. "The colors, the sounds...it's incredible."

Mystic knew well the feeling Xoxo was experiencing and was happy he had achieved it, but something was bothering him. How had Xoxo reached it? Mystic had to go through an intense state of self-reflection before seeing anything even close to what Xoxo was describing, so was it possible he hadn't had anything to do with this?

His desire to find and talk to Freedom was growing. He

felt in need of an explanation and a few kind words of reassurance.

"What's wrong?" Xoxo asked him. "You suddenly look preoccupied by something."

"Huh?" Mystic said, "Oh, I was just wondering..."

"What?"

"How did I do it? How did I change your perception?"

Xoxo looked unsure and shrugged. "When I felt that Cocoon was loved and not alone, I felt I'd woken up from an ongoing nightmare. I felt that somehow we are all the same, all connected. And Coccon felt closer to me in that moment than ever before."

"So I *did* do it then," Mystic mused. "It all happened when I told you about love."

"I guess it was, yes."

Mystic felt reassured. Xoxo had told him exactly what he had needed to hear, and he felt proud. *It's certain, then. It was I who helped him; I do have Freedom's power!*

"Thank you for this, Mystic," Xoxo said.

"You're welcome," Mystic said. "I'm so happy for you—and for me, too!"

"Yes, I have a feeling it would have vexed you not to succeed in making me happier, wouldn't it?" Xoxo laughed.

Mystic gave Xoxo an embarrassed look, but Xoxo held up his hands.

"Don't worry, Mystic," he said. "I know you did it for yourself. You *had* to do it for yourself, or we wouldn't have achieved what we did here today."

"And you're okay with still not being free?" It seemed incredible that the monkey, who had been so entrenched in

237

his sadness and suffering, could have changed his perception as easily as he had.

"But I *am* free, Mystic," Xoxo said with a grin. "I'm free up here." He pointed to his head. Mystic suddenly understood what Freedom had said.

"You're free mentally," he said out loud, tasting the words in his mouth. "You're physically here, but mentally you are free to go wherever and think what you want."

"Of course," Xoxo laughed. "Isn't that what you were trying to do?"

Mystic supposed it was, but he hadn't really understood it until right now. He hadn't thought about it in terms of mental or physical, he'd just let his intuition carry him in the direction he knew to be right. "It's incredible," he whispered.

"Isn't it?" Freedom said, and they turned toward her voice. She was seated on a large rock a few feet past the bars, sunning herself.

How long has she been watching us? And did she ever really leave?

The idea that she might have hidden nearby, spying on them and making sure everything went well, was comforting. Not to mention the fact that she might have seen his adventure firsthand, his success!

Mystic couldn't wait to hear her congratulate and praise him for the great progress he'd made. He started to swell with pride.

LOVE

Freedom came inside the cage, and Mystic watched her every move with large, love-struck eyes. Xoxo giggled a little, but Mystic ignored him. He didn't want to miss Freedom's glorious entrance or see Xoxo's shrewd smile.

Freedom paced over to Mystic and sat looking at Xoxo. He felt her fur touching his, each strand almost crackling with electricity against his own. He lost all control of his emotions.

"What you experienced was beyond amazing, wasn't it?" Freedom wasn't looking at Mystic but only at Xoxo, with a great smile.

"Yes, it was," Xoxo said, much more subdued than normal, as if even he was awed by Freedom's presence.

"I'm very impressed by how fast you were able to reach this peace and joy, Xoxo," she said. "It wasn't an easy thing to do for you, especially considering your situation." She looked around the cage. "Many others with less to contend with don't want to accept that they alone can make themselves happy. They refuse to be responsible for their own happiness and change the way they see things. To be fair, this responsibility can really be intimidating, but it's also worth it. And *if* they finally accept that, most of them choose to take a long time to put it into practice."

"Well, it was really Mystic who—"

"But you, Xoxo, you did it in a heartbeat," she interrupted. "At first you doubted it was possible to be happy by voluntarily changing your thoughts, but as soon as you began to experience love, you dropped all your doubt and surrendered to your knowing, even though you couldn't explain it. You are very brave."

As Freedom continued to praise Xoxo, Mystic felt a sickening sinking in his stomach. *She didn't sit beside me because she wanted to be close to me; she sat beside me so she could ignore me.* And on top of that, she was only speaking of Xoxo's talent and progress.

He thought he should jump into the conversation, tell Freedom how he had helped Xoxo reach this awakening, but he was paralyzed by humiliation. She had never ignored him like this, and he wondered if he had done something wrong.

She seemed blind to Mystic's suffering, though. "What's so impressive is how quickly everything became clear to you. It's like it all just clicked at once."

"But I only did this thanks to Mystic," Xoxo blurted out.

"Oh, I know he did a good job," Freedom said easily. "Well done, Mystic." She turned and acknowledged him for the first time.

Before Mystic could even say anything, she had turned away, back to Xoxo and continued to praise him.

"But you are the one who had to let go of your belief that nothing could be changed, that misery was a permanent fixture in your life, and *that* is an amazing accomplishment."

Xoxo opened his mouth to say something else, but Freedom cut him off.

"Well, I really should be going," she said, standing. "I have much to get done today. I just wanted to come and congratulate you, Xoxo—you really deserve it."

"Thank you," Xoxo replied quietly.

"You both take care and be well." And like a flash, she was back through the bars and had disappeared into the brush.

Mystic burst into tears. The pain of being rejected by Freedom was too brutal for him to bear in silence. Xoxo rushed toward him and scooped him up in his arms.

"I know she's right," Mystic sobbed. "I know you had a huge success today, and I'm as impressed with you as she is."

"But I wouldn't have been able to do it without you," Xoxo said. "You're the one who helped trigger this amazing shift within me."

"I know," Mystic sniffled, the worst of his tears behind him now. "I helped you achieve that. You even told me it was something I said. So, why so little recognition from her about my part in it?"

Xoxo shrugged.

"Does she dislike me that much? I thought we were getting along so well."

"It's clear that she likes you," Xoxo said gently. "She doesn't want to show us just how much she likes you yet, but it's obvious."

"Then why did she ignore me the way she did?"

"I don't know, but I'm sure there's an explanation for it. Just look, if I hadn't been imprisoned in this cage, I would have never met you, and I wouldn't have found a way to feel better about life. Somehow it's all thanks to this horrible place—and you, of course."

"What does that have to do with me and Freedom?"

Xoxo smiled cleverly. "What if all of this is just an opportunity for you to find the courage to go and talk to her? To tell her how you feel? That you like her?"

Mystic couldn't help but feel Xoxo's enthusiasm. It helped to lift his spirits.

"Maybe she's even doing this to help you learn something," Xoxo said.

That caught Mystic's attention. Freedom had taught him a lot since they'd met, and he hadn't always understood her right away.

"Do you think so?" he asked, hopeful.

"I do," Xoxo said. "Maybe she was trying to stop you from being so shy around her and so impressed by her."

"That would be nice, but I'm not so sure," Mystic said.

But Xoxo seemed convinced enough for both of them. "We have the choice to choose what we believe. And I choose to believe that she wants you to react, so go and do it! React!" He jumped up and down on the spot, making a gleeful screeching.

Mystic smiled, which led to a laugh. It was amazing how Xoxo had changed in such a short period of time from a negative monkey to one with such life in him. His enthusiasm was infectious, and it energized Mystic to jump to his feet.

"Okay!" he shouted. "I'll go and see her then!"

"Hooray!" Xoxo grabbed the bars of his cage, using them to pull himself up off the ground over and over again. He was like a small child. They laughed.

Mystic waved goodbye while his energy was still high and set off down the same path Freedom had taken moments before.

-2-

Once outside the cage and by himself, he was terrified by the idea of confronting Freedom. He had seen her strict before (the time she had told Trembly to leave came to mind), and he didn't want to see her like that again. Especially not toward him.

I must be calm and careful not to accuse her of anything, he thought as he walked. *I don't want to upset her.* But even thinking about talking to her calmly worried him. He felt as though what he was doing was wrong and that, if he carried through with his plan (which had seemed so rational moments ago but now felt like complete lunacy), she would hate him forever.

Lost in his thoughts and walking quicker than he realized, he had already caught up with Freedom. She had been moving slowly and now was bent over inspecting a low-blooming flower with particular interest.

Mystic took a moment to assess the situation. If he kept moving forward, she would see him for sure, and then there would be no going back. She would want to know why he had followed her, and even if he made up a plausible lie, she would see right through it. The alternative was to just turn around now, slink back to the cage, and let the feeling of rejection fester. There was really only one option as he could see it.

But first, he wanted to take a moment and calm down. His heart was going crazy, and he wanted to look confident when they spoke. He was out of breath, his fur sticking up wildly from contact with the various bushes he had plowed through on his way after her. And of course, he was painfully aware of his shyness and his concern that he would disappoint her.

But after taking a few deep breaths, he found his concerns weren't good enough reasons not to talk to her. He remembered the way she had almost completely ignored him. *How could it get any worse than that? She's already disappointed in me, so what can I lose by talking to her?*

The shift in his thinking relieved the tension he had been feeling. *There's always a way to see things in a more positive light, isn't there?* He was feeling more energized. *I love it!*

He was eager to speak to Freedom now, so he walked on. She was a little farther down the path, moving in a very relaxed manner.

I have nothing to lose, Mystic told himself over and over. *And who knows, maybe she will be impressed by me for coming to share my feelings.*

His happy thoughts were coming with greater and greater ease. He was pleased. One positive notion gave birth to another and another until his entire mood was changed. It was like magic.

Before he reached Freedom with this newfound sense of conviction, she turned and sat on the path facing him, as if she had known all along that he had been following her.

It startled him, causing all his carefully planned words to

fall out of his head at once. He blurted out the first thing that popped into his mind.

"Hey, Freedom!"

"Hey," she said with a smile. She looked kind and approachable, not at all like the stern and disappointed teacher he had expected. It helped him to relax. "What can I do for you?"

"I just had to talk to you," Mystic said more quietly now. "I had to ask you why...why you treated me the way you did when we were in Xoxo's cage." He said it fast, worried that, if he hesitated, he wouldn't be able to get it out at all. "You behaved as if I was nothing to you." His eyes watered with the memory.

"Why did it hurt you so much that I gave Xoxo more attention?" she asked. "Hasn't he done something amazing?"

"Of course he did," Mystic said. "I never said he didn't. And I'm impressed with him, too. What he did and the speed with which he did it, especially in his circumstances...it's very inspiring."

"So why did it shock you that I gave him all the attention?"

"Because he didn't do it all on his own. I helped him get to that point!"

"And how did it make you feel, helping him like that?"

"I...I felt proud," Mystic said, a little confused. "Like I was floating on a cloud of happiness. I felt great and energized."

"So why did you spoil your incredible state of happiness because I didn't give you the praise you wanted?"

"I know you told me I shouldn't care one bit what anyone else thinks about me or how they judge the things I do," Mystic said, "but it's so challenging! It gives me so much joy to be praised by others, I need it to be happy! I love it!"

"What did Xoxo say after you helped him?" Freedom went on, oblivious to Mystic's fit.

"He was really happy," Mystic conceded.

"What else?"

"He told me that, without me, he couldn't have done it."

Freedom smiled gently. "Well then, haven't you received your approval? You've been recognized for the great kindness you did, and got the praise you crave from the one whose praise *should* matter the most."

"Yeah, but I wanted *you* to react the same way!" Mystic said a bit louder than he had wished to. He couldn't understand why Freedom didn't see how much he needed her support and how much her attitude was hurting him. "Because I care about what you think about me...what you feel about me and—"

"Mystic, do you realize that you're spoiling the best part of your entire day because one person—only *one*—didn't lift you onto their shoulders and carry you around in triumph?" Freedom sighed. "I hate to say this Mystic, it hurts me, but you might want to consider giving up on your dream of being happy. If the only way you can achieve happiness is by pleasing everyone on the planet, you're better off saving yourself the heartbreak and frustration of failing almost constantly."

"Why would I fail?"

She shrugged matter-of-factly. "Because you can't please everyone. The only one you can please is yourself."

Mystic realized Xoxo had been right. Freedom had seen what Mystic had done, but she had ignored him purposely to help solidify this idea. He sighed, embarrassed.

"You see how this need to please others puts you in jail, don't you?" Freedom said kindly. "It's the worst state of dependence you can be in. It's hell. You see it now, right?" She was speaking kindly and softly again. Mystic was grateful.

"Yes," he whispered.

"I know it's a challenging thing to learn and apply, but you really need to be happy for you first. Everything else is trivial."

"But you're not trivial to me!" Mystic said. "I love you too much for that!" He was blushing before the words were even out of his mouth, but Freedom just kept talking as though she hadn't heard or understood what he meant.

"I'm not saying that you can't have friends and care about what they think, but please Mystic, don't become *dependent* on what they think of you," she said. "Learn to love your friends without the need for the approval you should be getting from yourself. Love should be free of any kind of need or justification. Love unconditionally."

Freedom stood up, stretched greatly, and then walked slowly down the path, sniffing the occasional flower. Mystic fell into step with her. They strolled together in comfortable silence for a while before he remembered there was another question he wanted to ask.

"I know it's what I said that helped Xoxo reach his

happiness today—he told me it was—but I have no idea *how* I did it. I feel I'm beginning to reach the same power you have to give others pleasant feelings and happiness, but I don't know how I do it."

"You're doing nothing," Freedom replied dreamily. "It's the power of being able to do nothing and just let what will come to you come."

"But I did do something. Xoxo said so."

"Yes, but without *trying* to do it," she said. "You weren't trying to find the perfect thing to say, you just relaxed and let it come to you, didn't you?"

Mystic remembered the flow of words from his mouth and the joy that had come with them. It had been energizing and, best of all, easy.

"When you feel amazing like that, when you find joy and don't take things too seriously, good inspiration comes to you and makes you more valuable to yourself...and to others."

Mystic loved that. Since Bumpa left, everything had been about that—finding the power of happiness—and each moment he felt closer and closer to it.

He was feeling great. He was glad he had overcome his shyness and had come to Freedom to talk. In doing so, he had reached a new level of confidence he hadn't known he was capable of.

Now he could tell her.

He felt ready.

Now was the moment.

"Freedom?" he called.

I can't stop now, I have to do this for me. The idea that he was doing this for himself was exhilarating. He knew it would be difficult to be detached from her reaction no matter what it was, but it was something he needed and wanted to do, regardless.

It has to be now. If I don't do it now, I never will. It must be now!

Freedom faced him once again, her green eyes soft and piercing. Mystic felt himself shrouded in shyness. *Oh what am I doing?*

"Yes?" Freedom asked.

"I...well, I mean, I..."

Freedom sat and watched.

It's as if she knows what I'm going to say, Mystic thought. *She knows I need to take my time, and she's not going to rush me. I feel safe with her, like I'm the only important thing in the world to her.* That gave him the courage to forge ahead, even though his paw pads were sweating horribly and his heart was fluttering in his chest.

"It hurts when you leave," he said finally. "And I miss you when you're not around." Freedom hadn't moved. She was breathing evenly with the same slight smile on her lips. He felt no embarrassment now as he watched her delicate features. He could have stayed watching her like that all day.

"You're beautiful, graceful..." he sighed in a love-struck voice.

Freedom said nothing, but her emotion was written

clearly on her face. She closed her eyes for a moment, as if experiencing extreme delight with each word Mystic spoke.

"I think that...that I'm in love with you," he said with a slightly shaky voice. "I love you, Freedom." He felt like fainting, as if what had just happened was a dream he couldn't quite get a grip on. What would she say?

But then he remembered that, even if she didn't say it back or feel the same way, he must be happy with himself for having told her. He had taken a step to increase his own happiness, and that, as Freedom had just explained, was the only important thing. The rest was trivial.

And besides, I don't have to hide the way I feel anymore. I've shared my feelings with her, and now everything is out in the open. I feel lighter. Freer.

"You're amazing, Mystic," Freedom said after a moment. "I so admire everything you've done and everything you want to do. You're a very noble cat." And with that she stood, walked the short distance to where Mystic was sitting, dumbstruck, and kissed him lightly on the lips.

Mystic's mind went completely blank for a moment, but when thought returned a short time later, he was grinning goofily from ear to ear. It really hadn't mattered to him if Freedom felt the same way. *But I am so, so glad she does,* he thought.

Mystic and Freedom walked side by side, smiling at each other and laughing. From time to time they stopped and nuzzled in a show of affection.

Mystic was in heaven. He was in love, and he was loved.

All of this made him think of Xoxo, who had lost his love

Cocoon, and what he said he'd felt.

"How do we know if what Xoxo felt about Cocoon was real?" he asked. "He said he could feel her all around him and that she was happy and loved."

"We can't know," Freedom said. "But what we do know is what he felt was real to him, and *that* can't be denied. Just because we can't perceive it, doesn't mean it can't be real. Xoxo believed it so strongly that it totally transformed him, so who knows?"

"So, you believe we all have our own realities?"

"It does feel that way," Freedom said. "To me, everyone has their own beliefs that help them to be a happier individual. And it's none of our business to judge or to impose our beliefs because we think they're better."

"Just because they are better for us, doesn't mean they'd be better for them," Mystic said in a flash of understanding.

"Yes!"

"So we can inspire others with our beliefs, but we should never try to impose them on anyone else."

"Exactly!" Freedom exclaimed. "I think everyone should be free to believe what they want and live in peace with each other."

"And be happy!" they finished together and laughed.

They were flying on a cloud of romance. They once again nuzzled together, joyously waving at every animal in the park they passed.

As they came up to Lili and Lulu's enclosure, the giraffes let out twin screams of pleasure.

"Come in here, you two!" Lulu shouted.

"Yes, come and tell us what you've been up to!" Lili

said.

Freedom and Mystic ran into their enclosure and told the story of what had happened since they'd last seen one another. Lili and Lulu were impressed and congratulated Mystic for the progress he'd made. They expressed their extreme happiness that he and Freedom were together. Mystic and Freedom entwined their tails and laughed.

Lili watched with amusement. "You two really are very sweet," she said, and Mystic felt overwhelmed with joy.

They talked a little more with Lili and Lulu, but before too long had to say their goodbyes. Mystic didn't want to leave Xoxo alone, not after the intense morning they had had together. He wanted to make sure he was still doing all right.

And to Mystic's great joy, Freedom decided to tag along.

-4-

As they approached Xoxo's cage, Mystic and Freedom heard laughter and voices chattering away happily. They sped up to the end of the path and turned right to face Xoxo's cage. The spectacle before them was beyond anything Mystic could have imagined.

Only two days before, Xoxo was a lonely and deeply sad monkey with no hope within him. Now this same monkey was in his cage, entertaining a sizable crowd. All around Xoxo were happy animals—birds, lizards, cats, and all sorts of rodents—laughing along with him as he jumped energetically from bar to bar. Mystic couldn't believe this was really happening!

"There he is!" Xoxo shouted from the top of his cage.

"It's Mystic, the friend I was telling you about!"

All the gathered animals turned and looked at Mystic, who was taken aback by their sudden attention. To his great surprise, he saw the group of wild cats and among them Dusty and Tiger. They winked at Mystic and waved.

Mystic looked at Freedom and she nodded.

"Go," she said with a smile.

He trotted over to Xoxo's cage.

"I told everyone here how you helped me!" Xoxo shouted. "How you never gave up on your belief that I could find happiness in here!"

Mystic smiled, his eyes shining with pride. He couldn't have asked for a better experience.

"And look!" Xoxo continued happily, leaping to another bar and dangling from it. "Look at all the friends I have now! You did this!"

"I didn't do it," Mystic said. "It was both of us. We did it together. *We.*" Saying this made him realize how sharing the accomplishment was giving him even more joy than if he had taken all credit for himself. All of this was possible thanks to his willingness to practice feeling good for himself no matter what. Thanks to this, he was able to share his success with Xoxo, which compounded the joy he was already feeling.

Mystic jumped happily through the bars. His feet had barely touched the ground on the other side before Xoxo scooped him into his arms and lifted him over his head like a trophy. Mystic and everyone watching burst out laughing.

Once Xoxo put him down, Mystic surveyed the crowd with a sense of awe. "How did all of you end up here?" he asked. "What happened?"

"I heard some noise," said a fat little chickadee in the back. "I came to see what it was, and Xoxo was jumping crazily around in his cage. It was too funny to stay away!"

"It was the same for me," giggled a little woodchuck.

At once everyone spoke at the same time, telling a similar story. They had heard Xoxo's joy and been compelled to come to him.

Mystic was stunned. It was the second time he had seen clearly that negativity and self-pity weren't the best ways to get attention from others. Happiness attracted happier attention, whereas negativity only attracted Trembly.

It was truly incredible and awe-inspiring. *Now that I've changed, I wonder what my relationship with my friends will be,* he thought. But he could sense the answer. It would be much easier and lighter than it had been before. There was something exciting about that. He'd only experienced holding others captive with his misery, but Xoxo's display today was truly inspiring.

"What are you thinking about?" Freedom asked quietly. She had walked up behind him as he was looking over the crowd.

He jumped and spun around. For a moment he had forgotten she was there. A feeling of shame crunched his chest.

But Freedom was smiling back at him.

"Freedom, I'm so sorry. I was so consumed by my glory that I forgot you were..."

"Shhh," she whispered and placed a paw on his mouth.

"But you should be upset."

"No," she laughed, taking her paw away. "Do you really think I love you just so you can pay attention to me, because of what you can do for me? That wouldn't be love. Because love is unconditional."

Mystic was once more astounded by the beauty within her. She wanted to be responsible for her own wellbeing and didn't want him to have any power over it. He greatly wanted to master this way of being as well. It made everything so simple and fun.

"You must be from another planet," he said softly, "but no matter what you say, I'm still ashamed of my behavior. You're the real hero in here, not me." Without her, he would never have given a single thought for the monkey who was now jumping and hooting in his cage like a lunatic.

"You're sweet," she whispered and rubbed her nose against his cheek. "Thank you."

Mystic looked in her eyes, letting his heart melt with hers, and kissed her.

After their moment of tenderness, Mystic turned to Xoxo, who was watching them with satisfaction, and mouthed the words "Thank you." Xoxo responded with a thumbs-up, which made Mystic smiled.

"You asked what I was thinking about," he said to Freedom.

She nodded. "And?"

"I was thinking about my friend Ulysses. I was thinking about what it would be like to be back with him now I've changed. Or even how things will be with Sarah and my family."

"Then why don't you go back for a visit and see?"

Mystic was shocked that Freedom could be so cavalier about the subject of their separation. "What about us?"

"What do you mean? You'll come to see me, won't you?"

"No, no, no," Mystic whispered, feeling the first pangs of panic building within him. "I want to be with you all the time."

"Oh Mystic," Freedom said, rubbing her nose against his soft gray neck.

"Why don't you come with me?" Mystic said suddenly. "I'm sure Jean and Pete and Sarah would welcome you."

"I am really touched, but I wouldn't do well in a house with humans. I need to stay outside. This is where I'm happy. And I need to keep spreading that happiness to others who can't find theirs, yet…as I did with you not so long ago."

Mystic knew she wouldn't change her mind; there was no use trying to convince her. Besides, he didn't want his love to create a jail for her. She had to be free, and he had to love her that way. It would only make things more difficult for them both if he tried to have it only his way. Rather than let his disappointment grow, he decided to let it go for now.

"Okay," he said. "But we need to meet—a lot."

"Of course we do," Freedom exclaimed joyfully. "I need to be close to you, too. I will—"

But they were suddenly interrupted by Xoxo screaming with terror. They turned and saw a scene of horror unfolding before them.

12

EVERYTHING IS FALLING INTO PLACE

Xoxo had been grabbed by a man and a woman wearing the blue outfits all the park's caretakers wore. They had found a way to grasp him by the arms and lift him into the air. He dangled there like one of Sarah's stuffed animals.

"They've sedated him," Freedom whispered with a hint of urgency. "We have to follow them."

Mystic's heart was thumping again.

"Don't let your fear overpower you, Mystic," she said. "Xoxo needs us—he needs *you*, right now!"

Mystic took a deep breath and nodded.

The two caretakers removed Xoxo from the cage entirely and carried him between them down the path. Freedom leapt through the bars, followed closely by Mystic. They crept along as close to the caretakers as they dared, always careful to stay out of sight and equally careful not to lose them.

The humans headed down a path unknown to Mystic. He had no idea what was going on. He felt sick, his stomach tight and queasy. It was the second time he was losing a friend!

Then he spotted Trembly by the path up ahead, smiling with toothy satisfaction.

Oh no, Mystic thought, but Freedom startled him and he lost track of Trembly.

"Look!" she whispered loudly, nodding toward the humans. The woman held Xoxo in her arms like a baby, while the man opened a crate in the rear bed of a red pick-up truck. The woman put Xoxo's head on her shoulder and gently rubbed his back.

"What's going on?" Mystic asked.

"I think that, for the first time, I'm witnessing the amazing power of happiness," Freedom said.

"What?"

"This is a good thing, I can feel it. Even better than that, I *know* it. Xoxo's change has brought him something good."

Mystic had no time to reply, Freedom was already walking toward the truck and the humans.

The woman holding Xoxo hadn't stopped cuddling him since picking him up, while the man was creating a bed for him with hay in the crate at the back of the truck. Another man wearing the same blue clothing appeared from in front of the truck.

"He's ready," the woman said happily to the approaching man. Mystic could feel in her voice that she was satisfied with something. He wished he could better understand her words.

"She said Xoxo was ready," Freedom whispered.

"You understand their language?"

"More and more."

Mystic was constantly being surprised by Freedom in all sorts of ways. She truly was incredible, but now was not the time to linger on that. "He's ready for what?" he asked.

"I don't know. We have to keep following them to find out."

The woman set Xoxo in the crate with extreme tenderness and kissed him lightly on the cheek. Mystic and Freedom exchanged surprised glances. Then the three caretakers climbed into the cab of the truck and started the engine.

"Quick!" Freedom said. "Follow me!" She sprang from her hiding place toward the truck.

Mystic didn't have time to consider. Freedom was running at full speed, so he followed her as fast as he could. The truck was moving, but slowly. They caught up to it and leapt into the bed, landing near the crate where Xoxo was starting to awaken.

Mystic was terrified. He didn't know what was happening to his friend, or where they were going, or even if he could do anything to help Xoxo.

"My intuition is telling me that everything is fine," Freedom said.

The truck went over a large bump, throwing everyone in the back off-balance. Xoxo screamed. He was fully awake now.

"What's happening?" he shouted, trying to pull the bars of the crate apart. "Where am I? Somebody help me!" He was turned away from Mystic and Freedom, so Freedom ran around to face him.

"Hey, you're okay, you're okay," she whispered softly, but Xoxo was out of his mind with terror. He didn't see her, even though she was right in front of him, as if she didn't even exist. He shook the bars more and more frantically.

"What's happening?" he shouted.

Mystic couldn't stand Xoxo's fright anymore. He

jumped around the crate and landed next to Freedom. He called to Xoxo in a soothing voice. Xoxo didn't see him, either.

It was such a joy to see him alive and happy. Why did this have to happen now? To see Xoxo's despair is worse than experiencing my own.

Mystic hadn't known before whether or not he would have been able to help Xoxo out of this situation. Now he was almost sure he wouldn't. He felt useless and powerless. His throat tightened with every scream Xoxo uttered. It was horrible.

And then Mystic saw something that made him shudder. Trembly was sitting on top of Xoxo's crate, looking vibrant, happy, and larger than life.

Oh no, not him.

Xoxo, who had not been able to see Mystic or Freedom, seemed to know that Trembly was there. He tilted his head back and gazed at the cat, who was staring down at him with malignant eyes.

"No!" Mystic screamed. He ran back and forth along the length of the bars, trying to get Xoxo's attention. But Xoxo's eyes were completely held by Trembly's. "He's not your friend!" Mystic shouted. "He's your worst enemy! He's your fear, your lack of hope, your negativity—"

Mystic was struck by what he had just said. *Fear, lack of hope, negativity...That's exactly what I'm feeling, too. There's no way I can help Xoxo when I'm feeling like this!*

He was surprised to see Freedom sitting a little way away by the side of the moving truck, smiling and breathing deeply.

"How are you able to do that?" he said. "How can you find a way to not lose control in this situation? How can you believe that all is fine and feel good about what's happening?"

"Because I trust my first intuition," she replied quietly. "I don't let my mind or whatever is happening right in front of my eyes tell me otherwise."

Mystic found himself shaking his head in disbelief. What she was saying was too hard to accept.

"I like to always go with my first good feeling," Freedom explained. "The one that comes so fast that most of us don't notice it. It comes fleetingly, and just as quickly it's gone. It's the one that makes you feel that everything is going to be fine...that is, until the unpleasant emotions and ideas attack you right after. You know what that's like, don't you?" She giggled. "When fear comes to you and wants you to be scared and miserable even before anything has happened?"

"You think nothing has happened yet?" Mystic said, shocked. "It seems to me like a lot has just happened to Xoxo!"

"Well, he's not hurt, he's just being moved somewhere, and there's no way for us to know yet if it's a good or a bad thing. So, I choose to trust my first impression, which told me everything's fine. If you can do that, too, Mystic, you'll curb Trembly's power over you and you'll also help Xoxo. Because if he sees that you're not panicking, that you still have hope, it will inspire him to control his fear. And when you feel better, you'll become inspired about what to say to help him feel better too. Remember?"

Freedom was speaking softly, with love shining in her eyes, but Mystic sighed all the same. Of course, he knew all this. But it was much easier in theory than in practice. And now was the worst possible moment for it.

But his thoughts were cut off. Mystic saw Xoxo with his arm over his eyes, sobbing. Trembly sat on top of the crate, a vicious smile on his face.

Freedom is right. Nothing has happened yet.

Mystic took a big breath and felt more relaxed.

I trust her intuition. With this thought, he immediately felt a subtle joyful hope as he remembered the caretaker in the blue shirt gently kissing Xoxo on the cheek. He decided that he owed it to himself and to Xoxo to try.

He took a step forward and gave Trembly a look of defiance.

"You know," he said, looking at Xoxo, "the humans who took you from your cage and put you in this crate acted very kindly. Especially the woman. She carried you, rubbing your back to reassure you, and when she put you in there she even kissed your cheek."

Xoxo uncovered his eyes, which were watery and red, and looked at Mystic with what could have been hope. Mystic's heart leapt.

"Really?" Xoxo asked.

"Yes, really," Mystic replied. "She even told one of the men with her that you were ready. We don't know what she meant by that, she never said, but she looked happy when she said it. As if you had achieved something. Something really good."

Trembly had been listening to all of this with a smirk. As

soon as Mystic finished, he leaned over so that he was looking into Xoxo's eyes again.

"Don't listen to them—you're a fool if you do," he said. "You know how it's going to end, you've dealt with it before. It's just going to be even more suffering when you finally come back to reality."

Xoxo lowered his eyes and looked at Mystic again. "I wish I could believe you," he told Mystic. "But I can't."

"Haven't I helped you to feel amazing before?" Mystic said, trying to keep the exasperation he was feeling out of his voice.

"Yes," Xoxo said hesitantly. "But now the situation is different."

"It will *always* be different, Xoxo. At least on the outside it will be. Inside it will always be the same. You can believe that all is fine, or you can choose to believe in your fear and give away your life to Trembly." Mystic felt joyfully powerful again and couldn't stop talking. "Maybe in some situations, for a while, you won't be able to control your emotions, but after the initial shock, you *do* have a choice. Especially when nothing really bad has happened to you yet to justify a lack of hope."

Xoxo said nothing, but his breathing had slowed to a normal pace. He looked much calmer than he had since the caretakers had nabbed him, almost relaxed. Mystic chanced a glance at the roof of the crate. Trembly was gone.

Yes! he thought happily. Freedom winked at him, and he felt a sudden wave of euphoria. He wanted to jump and dance around but managed to keep it inside. The focus shouldn't be on him but on Xoxo.

He wanted to go on, to keep reaffirming to Xoxo that

everything was going to work out, that all he had to do was to keep thinking positively, but the truck came to an abrupt stop, startling everyone.

-2-

Mystic had been so consumed by what was happening with Xoxo that he hadn't paid attention to anything else. He had no idea where the truck had taken them. He jumped on the edge of the tailgate and looked around, trying to get his bearings. It was no use. He had never been here before. They were at the end of a narrow street surrounded by high buildings made of red brick.

The engine died, leaving them in silence. Mystic glanced at Freedom with urgency in his eyes. He saw the same urgency in hers and read what it meant without her having to say anything. They must hide.

Xoxo was looking worried again, but to his credit, it wasn't the same panic it had been before.

"We have to hide," Mystic whispered loudly. "But we're not leaving you! We'll follow as closely as we can. Just remember to keep thinking about all kinds of positive outcomes for this situation, okay? Don't lose faith!"

Xoxo nodded. His expression wasn't the face of relaxation, but Mystic saw Xoxo's determination to try and felt pride.

"Let's go," Freedom whispered. She was at the back of the truck, ready to jump. Mystic joined her. He turned back and smiled at Xoxo, who was working hard to smile, too.

The truck doors were opening.

268

Mystic and Freedom jumped off the back of the truck in tandem, and once they hit the sidewalk, hid behind a garbage can standing not far away. They popped their heads out around the sides and watched.

The two men reached the back of the truck and pulled the crate toward them, while the woman went to a building and opened a door. She placed a large rock in front of it to keep it from swinging shut.

Freedom tapped Mystic's shoulder to get his attention and nodded toward the open door. "We have to get in there before they close it!" she whispered.

"Okay!" Mystic replied with great confidence, which surprised him. It was as if her positivity and confidence were contagious. He felt tremendously powerful and intensely alive.

The men were walking side by side now, carrying Xoxo's crate between them. It was now or never.

"Get behind the one on the right, and I'll follow the one on the left," he said, inspired. "That should keep us hidden from the woman, and we should be able to get in with no problem."

"Okay, let's do it!" The playfulness in Freedom's voice was hard to miss. Without another word, they ran from their hiding spots and fell into step behind the men.

Xoxo had seen them but made no indication other than a quick acknowledgement with his eyes.

And before Mystic even knew it, they were through the door, in a long corridor with a pile of boxes stacked along the wall to their left. He glanced at Freedom, who nodded, and they darted behind the boxes at once, just in the nick of time, as it turned out. No sooner were they hidden, than the woman turned to kick the stone back outside and the door swung shut. If they had remained behind the men, she would have seen them for sure. Mystic was proud of his intuition.

The humans continued down the hallway toward two large silver doors at its end, which sprang open on their own. The three people took Xoxo inside a small cubby of a room and stood waiting. The doors slid closed, followed by a low humming.

"What happened?" Mystic hoped Freedom would have an answer, but she had already left her hiding spot and was heading down the hallway toward the silver doors.

"I have no idea," she said.

Mystic followed and sat beside her, staring at the enigma before them.

"Something is moving behind those doors," he said after a moment. "I can hear vibrations and feel it in my paws."

As they scrutinized the doors, looking for a way in, the doors began to part. Freedom leapt to the left, Mystic to the right, and they stared at each other across the distance that now separated them. Freedom wore a huge smile, and for once Mystic felt the same enthusiasm. However scary all of this might be, it was a great opportunity to move forward and find Xoxo.

The cubby behind the door wasn't empty, though. The three keepers were there, the woman in front followed by the two men. Xoxo was nowhere to be seen. None of them noticed the two cats on either side, and they proceeded toward the door through which they had entered the building.

Making sure that no one was watching, Mystic and

Freedom ran between the two sliding doors and into the room beyond.

The situation was terrifying, but Mystic didn't feel terror. He had chosen to focus only on the positive aspects: he was safe, he was with Freedom, and of course, the joy Xoxo would feel when they found him.

"Now what?" he asked.

Freedom shrugged and smiled. "I don't know. Now we wait and see." For the first time, her relaxed answer didn't bother him. He was beginning to trust his intuition as Freedom always did, and it was a very freeing thing. He was enjoying this newfound sense of calm, when the lights overhead went off, plunging them into darkness.

And like that, all his positivity was replaced by apprehension.

"We're lucky we can see in the dark, aren't we?" Freedom said lightly beside him.

"Yes, we are." Mystic laughed at her unflappable positivity. She was right. The lights going out didn't change anything for them; they could still see just fine. Nothing at all bad had happened. He breathed easily again. Everything had gone silent. No, not everything. From far off Mystic could hear something.

"Do you hear that?" Freedom asked, and Mystic nodded.

"It sounds almost like Xoxo screaming something, but like a lot of Xoxos, and that's not possible, is it?"

Freedom shrugged. "That is what it sounds like."

Both had stopped talking and listened to the sound. There was no fear in the screams, just loud exuberance, as if a troop of monkeys were all chattering excitedly with one another,

271

each louder than the next to be heard over the commotion.

The lights came back on all at once, the humming started up, the floor vibrated, and the small room lifted into the air.

"It's moving!" Freedom said excitedly.

Mystic nodded as the box rose, reiterating in his mind that everything was fine and that this was all just an opportunity to find Xoxo. He was alert on his feet, ready to jump. A moment later, when the room slid to a stop and the doors began to open, that's just what he did. As they had when they'd been in the hallway, Mystic jumped to one side and Freedom the other.

Four men entered the room, chatting back and forth loudly. Freedom and Mystic lost no time. They nodded to each other and leapt out of the room at the same time, hoping their presence would continue to go unnoticed. But the hallway into which they ran was full of people. They had barely made it a few feet when a voice shouted, "Hey!"

Neither of them looked up. An opening with fewer people lay to the left, and they darted that way, weaving in and out of a forest of legs and reaching hands as people tried to grab them. They avoided them all, some by the skin of their teeth, and made it through to the other side, but what they saw was dismaying. The hallway ended abruptly in a wall.

Mystic's hope started to fail as his throat tightened and his heart pounded. *It'sokayit'sokayit'sokay,* his mind babbled.

"The hole up there!" Freedom shouted.

Mystic snapped his head up at the sound of her voice. Near the top of the wall was a large rectangular hole. He had

272

seen them before—usually, they had a covering over them—but this one did not. He had never jumped that high. His mind tried to tell him he couldn't do it, but he refused to lose his confidence again.

"I see it!" he shouted back. "I can do it!" The energy with which he shouted helped to convince him that he actually *could* make it. He felt hope return.

They reached the bottom of the wall at the same time, and without further thought, coiled and sprung upwards with as much strength as they could. There was just enough space for them to squeeze into the vent side by side. They landed, spared a moment for a giddy glance at one another, and resumed running. Freedom laughed and screamed joyfully. After a moment so did Mystic.

After the threat of danger was gone, they slowed to a walk, working their way farther into the tunnel. The deeper they went, the louder the monkeys became.

"We're getting close," Mystic said. "I hope Xoxo is there."

"I'm certain he is."

"Of course *you* are," Mystic snorted with laughter. "I would have been dumbfounded if you'd said anything else."

After a while, they could smell the monkeys too, and Mystic was certain now that Xoxo wasn't far away.

"He's just there," he said. "I smell him! He's there!"

Mystic began to run again, and Freedom followed closely. When they reached the end of the tunnel, they came to another rectangular opening like the one they had entered, only this one was covered by a louvered grate. They crept up to it and looked out through the openings. They were perched at the top of a very high wall. That wasn't what astounded him, though.

Beyond the grate was an amazing sight, even better than he could have hoped for in his wildest dreams. Mystic's eyes sparkled with tears of joy, and Freedom rubbed her head against his cheek, purring.

-3-

Before them was an enormous space completely filled with sunlight, trees, waterfalls, and rocks. Many different colorful birds flitted from branch to branch overhead, chirping happily to one another. The air was clean and carried on it the smells of nature and exotic flowers. And, of course, monkeys.

Opposite Freedom and Mystic on a branch at the same height was a bunch of macaques grooming each other in a long line. One of them was Xoxo.

"There he is!" Mystic shouted happily. "Help me with the grate!"

Freedom didn't have to ask what he meant. She lowered her shoulder to the grate beside him and pushed against it. They had to shove it a few times, but fortunately, it was flimsy. Whatever was holding it in place was no match for their resolve. Soon enough it popped out with a metallic screech and plummeted into a pool below. Thankfully, there were no monkeys in it and no one was hurt.

All the monkeys on the branch looked over at Mystic and Freedom. Xoxo's eyes lit up when he saw them.

"Thank you." Xoxo's voice was full of emotion. "Thank

you for saving me."

Mystic was momentarily speechless.

"You helped me change myself until I was ready for this," Xoxo continued. "I had to be in the right frame of mind for them to accept me here. I had to be happy before I could be amid more happiness."

Mystic felt Xoxo's gratitude, even from across the space.

"Thank you," Xoxo whispered again.

"Well, we should both be thanking Freedom," Mystic said. "She's the one who inspired me to choose happiness over the misery I was choosing before." He turned to her. "None of this would have happened without you."

She bowed her head to acknowledge this.

"Anyway, it's like I told you before," Mystic said to Xoxo, who was still watching him expectantly. "You did the hard part. I only did what gave me the most joy within."

As he said that, the other monkeys began screeching energetically and jumping around from branch to branch. Xoxo burst out laughing, got to his feet, holding one branch above his head and the other below his feet. He jumped that way, too, grunting happily.

Freedom and Mystic looked at each other in disbelief and laughed.

Xoxo's transformation into the monkey he was now was incredible. It made him think about Bumpa again. He had come to accept that he might not ever see Bumpa (and after they left here today, he might not see Xoxo either), but seeing Xoxo as happy as this made Mystic excited at the thought of Bumpa being equally happy. There was a sadness within him at the thought of losing two such friends as these, but his happiness for them was almost overwhelming. His intuition told him that Bumpa was living his dream just as Xoxo was.

And I guess I am, too, Mystic thought, looking at Freedom. Everything was just perfect. *Well...almost perfect.*

"How will we get home?" he asked Freedom.

-4-

Freedom and Mystic couldn't leave the way they had come in, or they would be caught for sure. There would probably be a whole bunch of people on the other end waiting for them.

"Only one way," Freedom said, smiling. "Straight ahead."

The enclosure where the monkeys lived was gigantic, but Mystic's keen eyes could see its end. Far on the other side was a wall of glass through which sunlight could shine, but the panels didn't go down to the ground. Below them was a gap just wide enough for a cat to squeeze through.

"Okay," Mystic replied, looking straight down to where the grate had plunged. It looked like a long, long way down. Much too far to jump without injury. The same was true of the nearest tree. There was no way they could be certain of reaching it, and a fall from this height was nothing to gamble on. "How do we get down from here?"

"We'll catch you!" said a monkey below Xoxo. "Jump, and we'll catch you!"

Mystic swallowed a hard lump in his throat.

"We're strong, we can do it!" said another monkey to

Xoxo's right.

"Okay!" Freedom said confidently.

"But what if they miss us?" Mystic said, worried.

"And what if we catch you?" Xoxo said with a wide grin.

Mystic laughed despite his concern. "Okay, okay," he said with as much confidence as he could muster. "Let's do it. A leap of faith!"

Freedom had already coiled her body back to gain as much momentum as possible. Mystic desperately wanted to reach out. Stop her. But before he could move a claw, she was flying through the air toward the tree like a gigantic black bird.

All the monkeys had moved to the end of their branches to be closer to where she was falling. They stretched their bodies out toward her as far as they could.

She fell past a branch where a young monkey was waiting. He almost caught her but missed. Then she fell through the tree toward the ground below, frantically trying to grab onto branches as they whipped past her. She passed three other monkeys who, despite their quick reflexes and nimble hands, each missed her as she plummeted.

"YOU CATCH HER!" Mystic screamed from the vent. "YOU SAVE HER! DON'T LET HER FALL!"

Just below Freedom was a wide gap between two branches, and there were two monkeys, one on either side of the gap. There was no way they would be able to reach her— she was falling near the center, much too far even for agile hands—but the monkey on the left acted quickly. Before Freedom could fall through the gap, he leapt into space, aiming for her small furry black body. He collided with her as gently as he could, knocking her toward the monkey on the right, who was ready to catch her as she flew toward him. He succeeded in grabbing her by the scruff of her neck.

Freedom let out a little scream as he snatched her from the air and managed to dig her front claws into the bark. She was safe.

Mystic collapsed to the floor of the vent, panting and whispering, "Thank you" over and over.

The monkeys erupted into cheers and screeches of celebration, jumping around happily. When Mystic thought he could stand again, he did. He saw Freedom and, a few branches below her, the monkey who had grabbed her out of the air. He was fine, sitting on a branch, clapping his hands. Freedom waved to Mystic.

Mystic sighed, but before he could lose the small amount of courage that had resurfaced, he coiled back and jumped out into the empty space between the vent and the tree. He was flying toward the tree when he saw Xoxo's face coming closer and closer to his. *I'm going to make it!* he thought ecstatically. Mystic's jump was leading him toward the branch where Xoxo was standing, arms stretched forward, ready to catch his light body. And before Mystic could think more, Xoxo's two agile hands grabbed his front paws, pulled him up, and set him down on the branch beside the blond monkey's body.

Mystic jumped with joy and rubbed Xoxo's face with his nose. There was another cheer of celebration from the surrounding monkeys. Soon everyone was making their way down to the base of the trees and over to the large glass panels.

Nobody said a word, as if they could all sense Mystic's resistance to the moment he would have to say goodbye to his friend.

"Isn't it stupid that I feel pain when I should be feeling joy? I should be happy for you," he said to Xoxo. "And for us," he added, looking at Freedom. "But instead of focusing on the wondrous things that have just happened and are surrounding me still, all I can think about is the pain of us being separated. It hasn't even happened yet, but I can already feel it instead of celebrating all of us being together right now."

"It's okay to feel hurt about that," Xoxo said. "I'm actually kind of happy that our separation hurts you. It means you really care."

At once Mystic felt lighter.

"He's right," Freedom said kindly. "But your pain isn't *just* that you're leaving Xoxo behind. It's amplified because you're judging yourself for feeling it. This is what really hurts you. It's important to accept all your emotions as they come without judging whether or not you should be feeling them."

"Yeah!" Xoxo said with a sly smile. "Who do you think you are to judge if your emotions are right or not? Look, it feels wrong to you that you're in pain? Well, it feels like the most natural thing in the world to me. I wouldn't have approved if you had been happy about it!"

Mystic giggled with Xoxo and Freedom as all the other monkeys screeched and jumped behind them.

Xoxo grabbed Mystic in his arms and squeezed him.

"I am the happiest macaque ever," he whispered in

Mystic's ear. "I had been dreaming day and night of what I've just gotten, but still my belly is in knots at the idea of having to let you go." He lifted Mystic up to his face so they were eye to eye. "Still, it's a beautiful emotion," he said, "a painful but beautiful emotion that translates to love."

Mystic felt a warm wave of love sweep through him. Yes, this painful emotion was actually quite beautiful.

"Thank you," he said to Xoxo, who was giving Mystic a final squeeze before placing him back on the ground.

-5-

After many embraces and goodbyes, Freedom and Mystic finally crawled under one of the glass panels. Mystic's throat was still tight, but he loved knowing that his sadness had its roots in the beautiful emotion of love. He accepted his pain and chose to look at it as something very positive.

I always have the choice, he reaffirmed to himself. He had the feeling he would be doing that for a long time.

Freedom walked alongside him, and even though Mystic felt as though there was much she would have liked to talk about, but she was being respectful of his emotions. He knew this the way that Freedom often knew what he was thinking, as if by telepathy. *I'm becoming more and more like her every day,* he thought and saw her smile.

They were making their way along the outside of the brick building, back to where they had jumped off the truck, when they heard a voice.

"It's the woman from the truck!" he whispered. "The

one who was carrying Xoxo!"

They had gone back, hoping against hope that the truck would still be there, and it looked as though luck was on their side.

"You're right!" Freedom said happily. "Let's go! We might get a ride back after all!"

They ran to the corner of the building and peered around it. The red truck was still there. No one was around it that they could see.

"This is amazing!" Mystic shouted as they ran to the vehicle. "This is *so* amazing!"

"Just the miracle we needed!" Freedom said.

They reached the back of the truck, jumped in, and it immediately rumbled to life. They looked at each other with delight. The caretakers had apparently been in the cab, ready to go. It couldn't have been more perfect timing.

"You see, when you begin to perceive the positives in life, miracles can happen. Real, physical miracles!" Freedom said.

Mystic was unsure. He had experienced his emotional responses to happier thinking, but physical miracles? That was a little harder for him to swallow. Instead of struggling with it, he decided to let it go for now.

Freedom didn't push the issue either, and as the truck rumbled its way along the narrow streets back toward the park (they hoped), they rode in comfortable silence for a while until Freedom finally broke it.

"Will you be rushing right home when we get back to the park?" There was no maliciousness or accusation in her voice, just gentle curiosity.

"Why do you ask?" Mystic's intuition was whispering something to him now, and not because he was angry or because he was afraid to listen to it. It whispered now because that's all it had to do to get his attention. What it told him was that Freedom had one more surprise for him that day.

"There's someone I'd like you to meet, if you can," she said.

"Someone who needs my help the way Xoxo did?" He'd gotten a sudden flash of Xoxo's cage in the park with someone inside it, someone much smaller than Xoxo. He couldn't see who it was, because it came to him so suddenly. He'd only seen a blur.

Freedom smiled. "I see you're honing your intuition. Yes, it's someone who needs your help."

"Then yes, I'd be happy to meet them." Mystic was elated that she trusted him enough to help someone else and that their adventure was not quite over yet. He knew that, at the end of it, he would be going home without her, and that was a little too hard to think about.

They had been so lost in conversation and their own thoughts that they hadn't noticed they were back in the park already. Mystic saw this only when he looked up and saw Lili and Lulu's necks craning over the trees in the distance.

"We're back!" Mystic said just as the truck came to a stop. It wasn't far from the old polar bear enclosure.

The engine cut off suddenly, and they were on their feet, running for the back of the truck.

"Come on, follow me!" Freedom said happily as she leapt down from the tailgate. Mystic followed her, once more running down the well-known and beloved paths of the park.

He recognized where they were heading, and as they got closer he became certain: Xoxo's old cage. But before they got there, Freedom stopped him with a gentle paw on his side.

"Shhh," she said, and they proceeded forward slowly, making as little noise as possible. She pointed. "There."

Mystic looked into the cage that was still just as depressing as it had been and saw a small figure curled up on the dirt. Whoever was in there was small and red—but not red like Trembly. This was a softer red, almost endearing. He realized that his intuition had shown him all of this, everything except for the cage's occupant.

And that's probably because I was taken by surprise. Maybe if I learn to expect it, I'll be able to see even more clearly! The idea was an exciting one and, as it turned out, one he didn't have to wait long to see realized. Another flash came to him just then, but instead of a static picture or a brief image of what might happen, he saw it as if it were happening for real, right in front of him.

He saw the little creature and himself playing as he had played with Bumpa not so long ago, rolling around on the ground in an enclosure that was much, much nicer than the one he was in now. All around the edges the children were lined up once more, their smiling faces craned forward, clamoring for a place to see the two of them playing. And with this vision, Mystic felt a great wave of happiness.

"He's cute," he said.

"He is," Freedom agreed. "And he needs your help. But

when he's ready."

"What's his name?"

Freedom just shrugged. "I don't think he has one, but the humans call him a red panda. That might be a nice way to introduce yourself to him when it's time. Give him a name that shows you care."

Mystic thought for a while and then decided to go with his first instinct. "What about Cutie?"

Freedom beamed at him. "I think that would be just perfect. But for now let's leave him be. He's had a very rough day and needs some time to himself."

And just as quietly, they reversed direction and headed back to the path.

-6-

After leaving Cutie's cage behind, they walked around the park for a little while. Mystic asked Freedom how they would contact one another so they could spend as much time together as they wished once he was back home.

"It's very simple," Freedom said, amused. "You just need to call me in your head, believe I'll hear you, and I will. And then I'll come."

Mystic looked at her with disbelief.

"It's true," she insisted. "Your intentions must be strong and direct. Feel the certainty that it will work, and it will!"

"And if I can't do that?" Mystic asked doubtfully. "Or if it takes me a long time to get the hang of it? How will I see you?"

"Don't worry, Mystic, I'll never be too far. Even if we're

285

separated physically, we're always together in here." She tapped her paw against her head.

Mystic remembered the almost magical way she had appeared when he was in trouble. "Is that how you always seemed to know when I needed you the most?"

"Of course! And see? I've always been there when you called me."

"But I *didn't* call you."

"Yes, you did, you just weren't conscious of it. But I felt you each time you needed me."

Mystic was once more in awe of her. "You're magic," he whispered.

"No, Mystic, I'm not. At least no more than you or anyone else. We all have this ability. Some, like you, just need to relearn it, but we all have it."

"I hate it that I'm different," Mystic said with mild annoyance. "Why do I have to relearn everything and look like a fool while doing it?"

"You may think you look like a fool, but I think you look like a *cute* fool," Freedom said with a smile. Mystic grinned ear to ear. "And don't forget, I was in the same exact place you are now. And look at me! I got it back!"

"So what's wrong with us then?"

"Nothing is wrong with us," Freedom laughed. "We're all different, and that's an amazing gift. It makes us powerful in the way that some others aren't, and that also means that some others will be powerful in ways we aren't. We all complement one another."

"So then we all have something to offer to someone else?" Mystic asked. "Something that will make their lives better? Happier?"

"Yes!" Freedom exclaimed. "Don't you love it?"

Mystic was thinking about his relationship with Sarah. He remembered how amazing he felt when she petted or played with him and how each time he had witnessed her feeling better as well. He actually couldn't remember a single instance in which either of them walked away from an encounter unaffected by it.

"Do you think we also share this connection with humans?"

"I bet we do!" Freedom said, confirming what Mystic's intuition was already hinting at. That confirmation wasn't the only reason he wasn't surprised by her excitement. It was also because she always seemed ready to believe anything that was positive and fun; she was driven by it. He thought that was just remarkable and loved her even more. She truly was an incredible creature.

Freedom kissed him tenderly on the cheek.

-7-

Mystic was alone walking through the park now. After the kiss, Freedom had gone off to help someone else who needed her, but before that, they had made plans to meet the following day.

Thanks to Mystic's experience with Xoxo, he knew how much joy it gave to help others attain greater happiness. But still, it had been hard for him not to beg her to stay.

It had been a long time since he had experienced pain like this, and to have the sensation back was almost unbearable.

"You see? I told you it never lasts!"

The voice was coming from the woods to his left, and came so suddenly that Mystic jumped. It was Trembly, of course—Mystic could recognize the smug satisfaction in it—and a moment later, the red cat stepped out onto the path.

"Hello, my friend," Trembly said. "I heard you calling for help, so here I am!"

"I never called you!" Mystic spat.

"You mean you didn't feel it? In your empty broken little heart? Ohhh, that's too bad." Trembly's grin transformed his face into a horrible mask full of pointy teeth. "Don't lie to yourself. You were in pain, and that's when you need me. You know that."

I can't let him in, Mystic thought, alarmed. *I must feel better! I must find a way! It's okay that I got hurt and scared for a moment when Freedom left, but I can't let that pain consume me. If I do, Trembly will become more powerful and transform into that horror he was before.*

At that thought, the image of Trembly tripled in size with hollow, empty eyes and a nightmarish mouth. He shuddered. The fear was beginning to return; he could feel it running rampant throughout his body.

Oh no!

"Oh yes!" Trembly shouted with great pleasure. "You can never escape pain! Never! If you'd only accepted that before, everything would have been so much easier! So why not do it now? Give up and accept that we're all doomed to this life of misery! You, Freedom, even Bumpa!"

Mystic knew rationally that everything Trembly was

saying was wrong, but his mind couldn't resist listening. His body shook with fear. He called Freedom in his head, shrieking for her to come, to rescue him. He visualized it the way she had told him, and for a split second, the image gave him a reprieve from his fear. He believed she might come.

But she didn't.

Trembly burst out in his nasty laugh, as if he had tasted Mystic's failure and found it delicious.

And what if Trembly's right? Mystic thought suddenly. *Happiness does feel like a fleeting illusion. Bumpa left, Freedom left...our happiness couldn't even last the short time we've been together.* He felt swallowed by anger. *Why did she have to do that? Why does she think that running off and doing what she loves is more important than staying here with me?*

"Because if I don't give myself what I need to feel good, then I won't be able to love you," Freedom said, appearing from behind Trembly, startling Mystic. "And the same goes for you, too," she added.

At once Mystic's anger was gone, consumed by a great burst of shame. He hung his head.

"Hey, you're okay now," she said, approaching him. "Trembly's gone."

Mystic was so embarrassed that those hurtful and selfish thoughts had crossed his mind and that she had heard every single one. "I can't look you in the eye anymore," he grumbled miserably. "I'm a loser."

"No, you're not," she said, covering Mystic's paw with her own. "You've just stumbled, like we all do."

"They were such awful thoughts," he said, angry at

himself for being so cowardly.

"Those thoughts weren't yours, Mystic. They just passed through your mind in a moment of weakness, but they don't belong to you. Don't take possession of them by judging them, thinking about them, or talking about them. Just let them pass through."

What Freedom had just said had succeeded in helping Mystic feel better, and he felt he could look at her again. He lifted his head. Trembly was indeed gone, and Freedom was watching him, her eyes full of kindness. It was the best thing he could have seen. To be thrown back into the negativity like that had been shocking and violent. For a moment, he had really believed he was doomed.

"It was so brutal," he whispered. "The pain when you left was bad, and then Trembly showed up and...it all went so fast. I just lost control."

"I know," Freedom replied, laying her forehead against his. The contact of her face against his own made him feel even better. "And it will happen again and again until you learn to recognize those moments of weakness before they arrive and to detach yourself from them before they gain a hold on you. When you can do that, they'll start coming less and less often and with less intensity."

"Can we ever get rid of them completely?"

"No," Freedom said, shrugging as if to say, *what can you do about it?* "Trembly will always be watching, trying to ferret out weakness in us. There will be no conquering him once and for all...And that's ok Mystic. You just need to stop catching your negative thoughts when they erupt, and let them become a part of you."

"It sounds horrible and like a lot of work," Mystic said, trying not to sound as discouraged as he felt.

"You'll do fine. If I can do it, anyone in the world can do it, too—trust me."

"Thank you for coming," he said.

She smiled. "I always will if I can."

-*8*-

They walked together to the edge of the park near Mystic's house. It felt to him as though it had been years since he'd been this way. He thought back to when he had taken Tiny to his home.

He smiled. *I was such a different cat then.*

"Well, I guess I should go home now," Mystic sighed.

"You *should?*"

"Yes..." Mystic was puzzled by her reaction, but his intuition told him he was about to gain some new wisdom, so he waited patiently for it.

"I never do things out of obligation or guilt," Freedom replied.

"But we have to sometimes."

Freedom smiled her wise, knowing smile again. "Acting out of guilt or because you feel obligated hurts."

Mystic could see she was enjoying helping him, and he realized he was, too.

"Ok then," he said, giggling. "Then tell me how I should...no, not should, how I can do that."

Freedom jumped up and down excitedly. "You know me so well now!" she said with glee.

291

Mystic was interested to know what she would say next. Every moment with Freedom was an exciting experience. He loved it.

"It's easy," she said at last. "I choose to feel happy about what I do, always. I find ways to want to do things I have to do. I look for what can bring joy or satisfaction by doing it. For instance, I used to dislike getting up in the morning. When I was sleepy, lying down, comfortable, warm, and cozy, the idea of moving was not appealing. It was a fight with myself to decide to get up. But you know what?"

Mystic simply shrugged and smiled. Listening to her was delightful.

"I have found a way to enjoy it now. To be excited about it." She giggled. "I keep my eyes closed, and I look for something I will do in my day that excites me. Even if it's an event that will only happen at the end of the day. I visualize it and feel the joy it will give me. Then I suddenly become eager to begin my day. And getting up is only a happy and enthusiastic experience. "

As always, Mystic was struck by the simplicity of it. It made sense.

"So?" Freedom asked. "Can you make going home a more positive experience?"

Mystic wanted to—the thought of home was very appealing—but there was Freedom to consider now.

"You know," she said, interrupting his thoughts, "even if you weren't going home, we still wouldn't be together all the time. We each have our own things to do. I have others I'm helping, and you have someone to help yourself."

Mystic hadn't really thought about it that way. He was

amazed by how Freedom could so directly and accurately address his concerns, telling him exactly what he needed to hear.

Going back home wasn't the reason he was feeling pain. His separation from Freedom was. If they were going to deal with separation regardless, it made it easier to come up with reasons he wanted to go back.

"I'm sad not to be able to spend all my time with you, but I'm really excited to see everyone at home," he said. "Especially Sarah and Tiny." The anticipation of his homecoming was building within him now. "Going home also allows me the opportunity to look forward to seeing you again and sharing news of my family with you, which I wouldn't have in the same way if we lived together. And with all my experiences out here, I can help my family to be happier than they are, as well as learn ways from them to be happier myself."

Wow, he thought, amazed at how fluidly all the positive thoughts were coming now. *It's the same situation as it was before, but there are an endless number of ways in which I can perceive it. And it always works! I love it!*

"Hooray!" Freedom shouted, jumping up and grabbing Mystic in her front paws, knocking them both to the ground. They lay there in a bundle of laughing fur.

"Thank you for giving me an extraordinary new life," Mystic said when the laughter died down.

"You're welcome," she said tenderly and gave him a kiss. "Come on. I'll walk you home."

They had just entered the yard behind Mystic's house when Mystic was struck by its beauty.

"Whoa," he said. "I never knew it was this lovely here. I must have been through this yard a thousand times, but I've never seen it like this before." He stopped, swiveling his head around, trying to take in everything at once. "Has it always been like this?"

"It has," Freedom said. "But often we don't see it, or we don't look for it, because our minds are too crowded with negativity. When we clear that away, the real beauty, *true* beauty, comes through."

Mystic was captivated by the incredible grass, vibrant and green, the trees a rich, creamy brown, the flowers each an amazing almost neon point of color. The smells made him nearly rapturous. "It's like what happened to me in Xoxo's cage."

"With continued practice, it will become easier and easier, like everything else," Freedom said. "The true beauty will shine through, not just of places but also of others and even situations. It's incredible."

They continued their walk through the yard, stopping from time to time to smell the flowers or to touch the feathery soft plants. Before long they were at the low wooden fence that separated this yard from Mystic's.

"This is where I go on alone," he said, smiling.

"I'll see you tomorrow or maybe even tonight," Freedom said. "And I'll see you every day and night that we can. We're going to have a lot of fun—you, me, and the others in the park. I'm so excited, Mystic, aren't you?"

Mystic had no room within him to be sad or even down. Everything waiting for them down the road was just fun. He didn't think he could even find a way to be depressed anymore. His life was like a fairytale. He felt blessed.

"I love you," he said, rubbing his nose against her cheek. "I love you."

"I love you, too, Mystic."

After saying their goodbyes and a goodnight kiss, Mystic jumped to the top of the wooden fence and, after a glance back at Freedom, slipped over the top.

-10-

Mystic walked through his own backyard, still amazed by the beauty he saw there. He was noticing things he never had before: the intricate elegance in a swirl of rocks along the fence, the soft gracefulness of Jean's lilies as they nodded in the breeze. It was heavenly.

He was halfway up the yard, moving more quickly now and angling for the cat door, when he heard Tiny's shrill voice screaming with joy.

"Mystic!" Tiny shouted. "Mystic!"

Mystic turned his head toward the sound and saw Tiny running toward him. He was surprised to see just how fast Tiny had blossomed in his short time here with Sarah, Jean, and Pete.

"Tiny! You're so grown up!" he shouted.

They ran toward each other and collided, bumping heads and collapsing into a pile of laughter. After disentangling themselves, they stood and jumped around with great joy.

That was when Mystic heard Sarah's voice. It was the most amazing sound. He hadn't even realized how much he had missed it until now. She was standing in the kitchen doorway, jumping up and down as he and Tiny were, screaming with joy.

Mystic and Tiny exchanged a happy glance and ran toward the house.

-11-

Mystic and Tiny lay beside one another on Sarah's bed. Sarah was on the floor, playing with her doll, chattering along happily to herself. Her excitement about Mystic's return had not yet died down, and it made him happy, especially now that they were upstairs resting comfortably on the bed. Sarah had insisted on carrying them both up at the same time, which hadn't been a pleasant experience for either cat, but Mystic had been surprised to discover that even that had brought him some measure of joy. Just the happiness on Sarah's face had increased his own pleasure.

As Sarah played, Tiny had asked Mystic to tell him of his adventures. Mystic did, speaking at length and telling everything he could. It was a wonderful way to reflect on everything that had happened. When he was done, Tiny stared at him wide-eyed, his mouth agape.

"So, if I choose to be happy, then only good stuff will happen to me?" Tiny asked. "All my wishes will come true?"

"I don't know, Tiny. It's what Freedom seems to believe, but—"

"So it's true!" Tiny exclaimed.

"No, not necessarily."

"But you just said that Freedom believed it!" Tiny protested.

"Well, she also made it clear that, just because someone says something is true, that doesn't make it so. Whatever we perceive is what we believe, and that makes us think it's the ultimate truth. But in fact, it's only *our* ultimate truth. There isn't just one truth, or even many, but as many as there are people and creatures in the world."

"Wow, that's a lot."

"Look at Sarah for instance. She's seeing things while playing with her doll that we can't perceive, so her truth of what's going on is very different from our own. And I'm sure Jean and Pete have a very different vision of the truth as well. They might all be looking at the exact same thing, but it's not really the eyes that see. It's the mind, and it's directed by whatever beliefs we have up here." He tapped his head for emphasis.

"So, if we decide to fill our minds with happy thoughts, then we'll see happy things around us?" Tiny asked.

"That's what I experienced."

"But what about when Xoxo fulfilled his dream?" Tiny persisted.

"I don't know, Tiny," Mystic replied honestly. "Freedom enjoys thinking that it was Xoxo's change of perception that caused his miracle to happen. She really does believe that."

"And you don't?"

"About that I'm not sure, but what I *do* know is that we should never judge anyone else's beliefs or vision of the truth. We should never try to impose ours on anyone else. Remember it's only *our* truth. *Our* way to feel better about life. It only concerns *us*. We can listen and share beliefs if that's what we want to do, but we should never argue and fight about them. If everyone could accept that everyone else has a different truth and way of thinking, then the world could be a very happy place for us all."

For a moment, the two cats said nothing, imagining such a perfect world where everyone was free to have their own beliefs. It would be such a happy place.

"Well," Tiny said suddenly, "I like Freedom's belief. It can't hurt. It can only help me to be happier, so I don't see why I would reject it. It's so easy to take others' negative beliefs, like life is tough and unfair, so why shouldn't I take a happy belief for once?"

Mystic smiled at Tiny. He understood that the little cat had been born with the instinctual knowledge that Mystic had had to relearn with Freedom during this last week. Tiny had simply never forgotten his instinct.

"Good for you," Mystic said. "And good for me to have the luck to have you as my family now." He purred and rubbed his nose against Tiny's cheek, which caused Tiny to purr, too.

Sarah, perhaps hearing the purring, turned toward them with a look of excitement and love and jumped around them happily.

"Happiness is contagious," Tiny whispered.

"Yes, indeed," Mystic whispered back.

The reunion with his family had been amazing. Mystic would never have guessed it could be so pleasant, and being at home with a new little brother was simply perfect. It was so much more fun than being alone.

Now he lay on the back of the sofa with Tiny in front of him sleeping soundly. The family was done with dinner (both Tiny and Mystic had gotten generous portions of wet food), and everyone was gathered in the living room, chatting happily and relaxing.

Suddenly, Sarah screamed, waking Mystic and Tiny up, and startling everyone else.

"Look!" she shouted. "Mystic's on TV!" She pointed at the screen as she spoke, jumping up and down with excitement. Mystic wondered why and followed her gaze. What he saw stopped him cold. It was him and Freedom in the enclosure with Xoxo and all his new friends! He got up and approached the screen, watching with wonder as he did.

"Look!" Sarah said, pointing at him. "Mommy, look! He knows it's him on the screen!" Jean and Pete tried to calm her down, but it wasn't easy.

Tiny walked up behind Mystic silently, his gaze held by the screen, too.

"Mommy! The black cat jumped, and the monkeys caught her!" Sarah shouted and bounced up and down again. "Oh, and now Mystic jumped and they caught him, too!" Mystic smiled, watching himself and Freedom leaping across such a large space (which looked even larger now he was seeing it from a different perspective). *It's easy to smile now, knowing that they'll catch us,* he thought.

Tiny was staring at the screen agog. "It's magic," he whispered. "You told me about it, and now I'm seein' it!"

Mystic laughed and turned back to the screen, wanting to see if there was more, but he no longer saw the monkey enclosure. Instead the image was of a large field with tall yellow grass rustling in the wind. Mystic's interest waned. He went to the couch to resume his nap, when Bumpa's voice filled the room.

He turned back to the screen, unsure what to expect. What he saw filled his heart to the bursting point. It was Bumpa. He was on the screen where Mystic himself had just been, walking out of the back of a truck in his lumbering gait that Mystic remembered so vividly. Another elephant walked beside him. They moved in unison, as if they'd known each other for years.

"Hello, Mystic," Bumpa trumpeted, facing the screen. "My intuition is telling me you can hear me now. I don't know how that's possible, but I always do what it says. I think you've probably learned a little bit about that by now though." Bumpa winked, and Mystic just stared at the screen, totally amazed. "I hope Freedom has helped you as much as I've dreamed of and even more," Bumpa continued.

Mystic began to pant. The emotion of seeing Bumpa again was incredible and intense. Tears welled up in his eyes. He had dreamed of this moment for so long, imagined it over and over, and though it wasn't as he had pictured it, the emotions were.

"Bumpa!" he cried. "Bumpa!"

"Before I left, I made sure that Freedom would take care

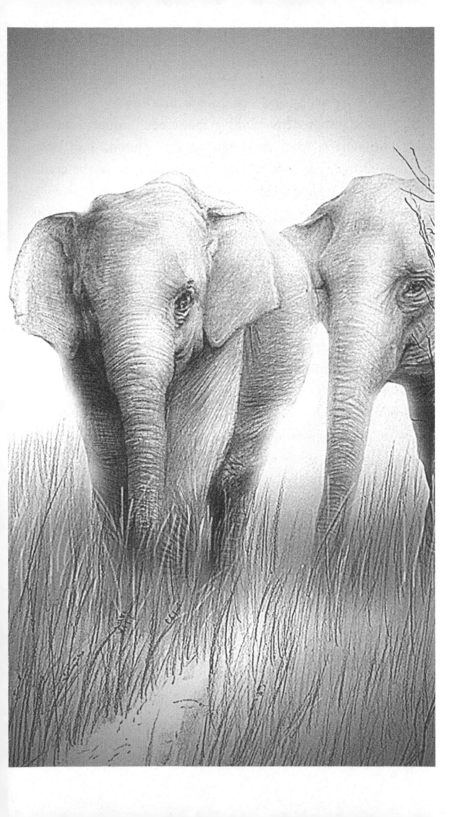

of you," Bumpa said as if he couldn't hear Mystic. "You deserve to be happy and free. Life is amazing."

Mystic watched his friend on the screen through a curtain of shimmering tears. He realized that Bumpa had been removed from the park and taken to a place where he could be free and thrive, just as Xoxo had been. *Somehow, Bumpa knew it was going to happen,* he thought, his heart overflowing with love. *He kept it a secret so we could enjoy all our time together right up to the end. Just like Lulu said. And before he left, he sent Freedom to me because he knew I needed help discovering what true happiness is. He sent her to me to help set me free.*

"Do you remember that night when I made a wish and said that I would tell you what it was when it came true?" Bumpa said. Mystic did. It was a memory he could now look on with joy in his heart instead of sadness. "This is what I wished for! It came true, and I am living my dream! I've never been happier in my whole life!"

I am so happy for you Bumpa. I am so happy that you are free and living your dream, I can hear the joy in your voice! Mystic hoped these thoughts would reach Bumpa somehow.

"I miss you, Mystic, and I think about you every day, but I trust that you are happy and free and experiencing how amazing life really is." Bumpa trumpeted loudly on the screen and his smile spread all the way up to his ears. "I am confident now that you understand when I tell you to surrender to what is happening and find a way to feel the good in everything."

Yes, Mystic giggled. *I do understand this Bumpa, and I am very happy...Freedom has given me the best gift of my life. I am alive today like I have never been before. And tomorrow I will be even more alive, and the day after tomorrow, even more than that. And it's all thanks to you, Bumpa.*

"I love you, Mystic," Bumpa said. "I love you."

Thank you, Bumpa. I love you, too, forever and always.

The image on the screen changed. Mystic stared at it for a little while, waiting to see if Bumpa would come back, but he didn't.

Mystic returned to the couch where Sarah was now seated, holding Tiny in her lap, petting him. Mystic climbed in beside his new brother and began to purr.

He looked out the window before settling down and saw Freedom there beyond the glass, a smile on her face. She winked and then jumped down off the sill. Mystic smiled to himself as he lay down in Sarah's lap.

He closed his eyes. *Forever and always,* he thought.

The End

NOTES...

Mystic and the Secret of Happiness is
Anne-Claire Szubaniska's first novel.

AUTHOR'S NOTE

When I was ten, I told my mother I would write a book about the painful experiences I had as a child. It would be about all the negativity I suffered and the people who had caused it. As it turns out, life had a better plan for me, I just couldn't see it yet.

As a young adult I struggled with anorexia, depression, and a hatred of life, all of which were manifestations of my deep-seated fears. Then one day, I read my first self-help book and found that the happiness I had known years before when I lived with my grand-parents was something I could have again.

This discovery led me on a chaotic journey, full of ups and downs as my fears and negativity tried to force their way back in, but I never gave up. Finally, I got a sense of what my inner joy was, and how I could achieve it in a sustainable way.

It was then that the intense desire to write about my experiences resurfaced, only this time I wasn't held back by the dark story of my childhood. This time I was inspired to write something positive, something easily accessible to all people; a story about a cat who had to endure his own troubled journey to discover the true happiness within.

Mystic and the Secret of Happiness was born.

ACKNOWLEDGEMENTS

Thank you my dear friend Andrew Herold for giving me the confidence I needed to write the story of Mystic.

Thank you Antoine for never giving up on me during the difficult times I had, and for inspiring me to keep going. Thank you for your patience when I greatly lacked it. And most of all, thank you for our love, without which I would never have been able to open my heart to Mystic's story.

Thank you to my mother who fell in love with Mystic's journey as soon as she read my first draft.

Finally, to my family who supported me in ways I had not even dared dream of.

If you enjoyed this book, I would greatly
appreciate a moment of your time
to leave a short review.
Your feedback helps other readers discover
this story and is invaluable to me
as a first time author.
Thank you!

Made in the USA
Las Vegas, NV
12 September 2023

77369914R00184